A
FREE
Nation in Our Land

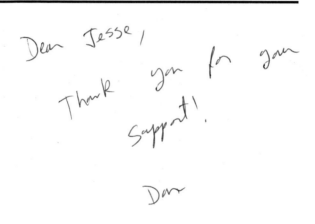

Dear Jesse,

Thank you for your Support!

Dan

DAN ILLOUZ

ISBN: 978-1-63323-866-4

TABLE OF CONTENTS

DEDICATION

To my parents,
who through their countless sacrifices
have made me who I am

INTRODUCTION

Israel is faced with more challenges than most countries. These challenges make it more urgent than elsewhere to take a deeper look into policy considerations before making rash decisions.

First and foremost are the security challenges that Israel faces. Ever since its establishment, and even before it, Israel was faced with existential threats. Before 1948, the Arab population attacked Jewish immigrants returning to Israel in order to stop the establishment of the state. From 1948 until 1973, Israel was faced with wars in which most of the Arab armies united in order to defeat the State of Israel. Israel won all of these wars, including the miraculous victory of 1967, when Israel liberated Jerusalem, Judea and Samaria, but knew that it would take just one loss to permanently defeat the young Jewish State. While Arab countries could afford to lose wars, each war was an existential threat for Israel. Since 1973, the enemies of Israel have changed their strategy and focused on terrorism, targeting regular civilians as a way to slowly defeat the Israeli spirit. This strategy has also failed, although it continues to make life in Israel more difficult. The Iranian attempt to develop nuclear weapons while sponsoring this very terrorism makes this threat ever more dangerous. The recent attempts to delegitimize Israel is a new weapon that the enemies of Israel have added to their arsenal in an attempt to prevent the Jewish State from defending itself.

On the diplomatic front, while Israel is making new relations with various countries and strengthening ties with allies, the threats of the BDS movement and of the delegitimization movement make Israel especially prone to diplomatic attacks from international organizations such as the UN bodies, from the European Union, and even from so-called allies who paternalistically want to force diplomatic solutions on Israel.

On the economic front, Israel is nothing less than a miracle. The start-up nation, which is itself a sort of start-up, went in less than 70 years from a country whose existence was considered a miracle to becoming an economic superpower that is part of the OECD. In a country with very few natural resources available, Israelis have used grey matter to create technologies that have already revolutionized the way we live.

However, internally, Israel is faced with serious economic problems leftover from the socialist policies adopted by Israel's founding fathers. Cartels abound in almost every sector; regulations serve as barriers to innovation and entrepreneurship; the cost of doing business is incredibly high; and tariffs ensure that prices remain high since international competition is also blocked. Strong unions ensure that any policy change remains almost impossible. The result? The gaps between the rich and the poor are high, the salaries are low, and the prices are high. It is very hard to live in Israel.

Internally, Israel has some serious challenges. The relationship between religion and state has yet to be defined in a country that is seen by most as the Jewish State—a concept that each group of people defines differently. The "Israeli culture", non-existent just 100 years ago, is developing at record speed in a uniquely multicultural way, inspired by the heritage of the Jews who were once spread across the world. These developments inevitably lead to birth pangs as people disagree about the right direction for the country. As this rich new culture develops, the old elites, used to defining culture and ideology for all, are trying to fight back by holding on to their sources of power, whether in the universities, in the courts, or in the media.

These are all serious challenges. However, when viewed from a historical perspective, the very fact that Israel has made it far enough to deal with these challenges is a miracle in and of itself.

Israel is, after all, one of the most unlikely stories to ever become reality. How many other nations do you know whose people have returned to their land after 2000 years of exile, during which time not only were they spread across hundreds of countries but also were constantly persecuted? The answer is simple: None.

How many other nations do you know whose people have managed to revive their historical national language, once considered for centuries to be dead? Here, too, the answer is simple: None.

How many other democracies do you know that were created as an oasis of democratic thought in a desert of despotism and managed to survive decades? A democracy under constant threat of war—a situation where democratic rights are usually put on hold? The answer, here, too, is simple: None.

The very existence of Israel is unlikely. Yet Israel has in a short time become a leading symbol of freedom, democracy and hope. The challenges it faces today— serious though they are—are much less than the challenges Israel has already overcome. Considering all this from a historical perspective brings complete faith in Israel's ability to rise and defeat these challenges.

The challenges listed above, and many others, were central to the columns I have written for the past few years in various newspapers. In each of my columns I have tried to analyze policy challenges affecting Israel according to a set of values. In the United States or England, these are considered "conservative values", while continental Europe would call them the values of "classical liberalism".

Since moving to Israel in 2009, I have been involved in various aspects of policy making. First, I was involved in civil society, promoting policy through public support. I then worked in the Ministry of Foreign Affairs in a role dealing with international law, before moving on to working with the Mayor of Jerusalem. I then went on to work as the legislative advisor to the Likud faction in the Knesset and to the coalition. This experience, that combines municipal and national levels, political and policy roles, gives me a unique outlook on policy making in Israel. In all of these positions I always tried to promote a conservative outlook in order to make Israel stronger, more successful and more prosperous.

The name of this book is taken from the national anthem of the State of Israel, *Hatikvah (Hope)*, that ends with the words "to be a free nation in our land", describing the great dream the Jewish people held in their hearts for over two thousand years of exile. This title was chosen because it manages to summarize in a few words the values that guided me when tackling the various policy issues I comment on in this book:

Free:

Freedom is the fuel of Zionism. Zionism is first and foremost the liberation movement of the Jewish nation. After two thousand years of exile under the rule of other nations, Jews from around the world came back to their own land and, through representative democracy, to self-determination. This reality leads me to strongly support a strong Israel which can defend its self-determination from outside threats, as well as to support a strong representative democracy opposed to any attempt to remove power from the people and give it to other, even if well intentioned, officials (including courts and bureaucrats).

On an individual level, Freedom is also the fuel underlying the free market. If one believes in Freedom, he must be opposed to useless constraints. Since legislation and regulation usually constrain people, then freedom lovers should, in most cases, prefer the free market to the paternalistic central planning of the state.

Nation:

Zionism is the national movement of the Jewish nation. While the post-modern world questions the necessity of the nation-state, Israel's existence is based on it. Where patriotism has become, in some circles, a negative term, I see it as one of the purest forms of human solidarity. The Jewish nation is also the proud bearer of a great tradition that brought to the world much of its values. The Jewish nation is an ancient, one that has survived thousands of years of attacks. It will also survive this post-modernist attack on national identity.

In Our Land:

The historic love story between the land of Israel and the people of Israel has been actualized through the State of Israel. Two thousand years of yearning have come to an end, and the Jews who were violently exiled from their land have finally been called home. However, it is not only historical justice that warrants Israel's return to its historical homeland, but also international law, as entrenched in the British Mandate. No other nation or people can lay equal claim to it. The whole land of Israel, including Judea and Samaria, belongs to the State of Israel, according to historical justice, legal rights and morality.

With these values in hand, we can examine every challenge facing Israel, from the Arab-Israeli conflict and the Palestinian question to economic issues and issues of religion and state.

In this book I try to provide a coherent and fresh perspective on the challenges facing Israel, based on these great values. My perspective is based on a complete faith in the ability of the Jewish nation to rise above present-day challenges, and I advocate a clear, hopeful message, based on conservative values and a prudent approach, as opposed to rash decision making.

I welcome you to send any comments or questions by email to dan@diconsulting.co.il in order to continue the discussion online.

ISRAEL AND
CONSERVATISM

A Conservative
Movement in Israel?

In the beginning of the 1980s, a new age began in international politics. Indeed, between 1979 and 1981, two major figures were elected leaders of important countries, in what was nothing less than a groundbreaking change in each country.

On one side of the Atlantic, Margaret Thatcher, the Iron Lady, was elected England's prime minister in 1979. Thatcher brought a conservative worldview with a strong belief in the free market, a strong patriotic feeling, and a realist view of international matters.

On the other, Ronald Reagan was elected in 1980 as president of the United States. It is hard to imagine today the extent to which his election revolutionized American consciousness. Since that time, every American election cycle has featured Republicans running in their party's primaries claiming to be carrying the torch of Reagan's principles. Until Trump, Reagan-style republicans also consistently won that nomination.

Reagan, too, brought a worldview that promoted a strong free market, a strong patriotic feeling, and a realist view of international matters.

In both cases, the conservatives who elected them did not regret their decision. Thatcher remained Britain's prime minister until 1990, for 11 consecutive years, the longest continuous period of office of any prime minister in the 20th century United Kingom. Reagan remained president for eight years, the maximum two terms allowed by American law, and his successor, George H.W. Bush, was elected to replace him, a sign of satisfaction with his predecessor's job performance.

The success of conservative politics

In both cases, we can also see actual achievements. If, at the start of their respective terms, communism was a real danger to the Western world, then the realism of these leaders helped them mitigate this danger, as evidenced by the quick demise of the Soviet Union.

On an economic level, before Reagan came to office, the American economy was in a state of "stagflation," stagnation in growth and employment, combined with inflation in consumer prices. The marginal federal income tax rate was 70%. The inflation rate was increasing by double digits annually and averaged 12% under US president Jimmy Carter. Annual GDP growth under the previous administration had been less than 1% (0.6). National unemployment was over 10%. The American economy, in fact, had not been worse since the Great Depression of the 1930s.

Reagan promoted free-market economics, drastically reducing taxes and government spending and advocating for deregulation. The results were immediate. His economic policies saw a reduction of inflation from 12.5% to 4.4%, and an average annual growth of real GDP of 3.44%.

Thatcher implemented similar economic policies. Inspired by Ludwig von Mises and Friedrich Hayek, she championed mass freedom to innovate over bureaucratic economic planning.

Thatcher cut the income tax on the highest bracket from an incredibly high 83% to 60%, while also lowering taxes for the less wealthy. She cut government spending in almost all areas except for defense and police spending.

While early on, the reforms did not affect Britain's economy, which continued spiraling down into a recession, by 1983 the economy was improving. In 1987 the inflation rate was as low as 4%, down from an earlier high of 21%, with the economy growing at a rate of 5%.

Most importantly for our discussion, Thatcher had a lasting impact on British policy and politics, as well as on public discourse, with a British Labor Party politician, Peter Mandelson, complimenting her by stating in 2002 that "we are all Thatcherites now."

The Begin revolution

In Israel, as in the United States and England, during the early 1980s a similar, yet different, political revolution occurred.

The "Mahapach" (shake-up in Hebrew) came when Menachem Begin was elected prime minister in 1979. Here, too, the revolution came from the Right, at the expense of the Left. The Likud, the "liberal national party," beat the socialist Mapai Party.

Sadly, here in Israel, despite the political revolution, it's hard to talk about a real change in government policy. While some advancement has been made toward free-market policies, and while right-wing governments have won successive elections, the public discourse in Israel is still one that promotes social-democratic values and utopian land concessions.

Today, 35 years after that political revolution, Israel is still led by the Left's worldview. On a diplomatic level, even a right-wing prime minister from the Likud is forced to accept the Oslo framework, which was promoted by the Left as a diplomatic solution for the Israeli-Palestinian Conflict, and to recognize the two-state solution advocated by that framework.

On an economic level, even a prime minister like Benjamin Netanyahu, who is a known proponent of the free market, must, in every new election, demonstrate some socialist achievements, despite being inconsistent with his own worldviews, in order to get reelected—from different kinds of subsidies to the expansion of government services.

Netanyahu is clearly a man with strong liberal economic values and a deep feeling of nationalism—what Americans call a conservative worldview. He is also one of the most powerful prime ministers to have ever served Israel. If he is unable to embed conservative values into Israel, it only underlines the difficulty of such a task.

Israel should be a more conservative country

Israel seems to be a place where conservatism flourishes. On an economic level, the ethos of the country is based on innovation. Israel is called the "Start-up Nation," and people value entrepreneurship. This should mean that free-market principles would be popular in Israel.

On a moral level, Israel is a country that traces its roots back to biblical times. As Leo Strauss, a conservative philosopher, wrote in a letter about Israel and conservatism, "Whatever the failings of individuals may be, the spirit of the country as a whole can justly be described in these terms: heroic austerity supported by the nearness of biblical antiquity."

As an outpost of democracy, surrounded by enemies seeking its destruction, Israel should be encouraged to move away from utopian visions and embrace a realist view of international relations.

According to every single layer of conservative philosophy, the conservative movement should be growing in Israel.

In addition, there are also sectors of Israeli society that should be fertile ground for the growth of the conservative movement.

The revisionist movement started by Ze'ev Jabotinsky was based on values almost identical to the conservative movement: an opposition to socialism, and realism with respect to international relations.

The religious-Zionist movement, while today largely based on the Hegelian philosophy of Rabbi Abraham Isaac Kook, still has some strong conservative tendencies. For example, Kook's philosophy itself shows great respect for historical processes, a foundational principle in conservative thought. Religious Zionists also tend to be aligned with the Right with respect to international relations.

Finally, the Sephardi community in Israel—which on the one hand is very respectful of tradition, as conservatives are, and on the other hand was the victim of the socialist policies of Mapai and central planning that preferred the Ashkenazim to their Sephardi counterparts—should also be prone to embrace conservative philosophy.

The need to invest in public discourse

If the record of conservative politics is so positive, if Israel's current prime minister is an ideologically conservative politician, and if Israel has all the ingredients to be fertile ground for the growth of a conservative political movement, why is it that such a movement has yet to emerge?

The answer is simple: Before the conservative movement emerged in American politics, it materialized in American public discourse. Various vessels enabling the communication of conservative thought, including newspapers such as the National Review, and figures such as Leo Strauss who were influential in academia, emerged. Also, before it succeeded in winning an election, the conservative movement also lost elections led by courageous politicians who were not afraid to campaign with an ideology not yet ingrained in the American mind.

For a conservative political movement to emerge in Israel, the public discourse must first change. Incentives must be created for politicians to act conservatively. This can be achieved by pressure groups, and by changing the general public discourse. Once the public discourse changes, the political world will follow.

Therefore, those who want to see a conservative movement rise in Israel, for the good of Israel, should work toward changing the public discourse to embrace free market principles, realist international relations, and conservative political principles.

Understanding
Netanyahu's Mind

Prime Minister Benjamin Netanyahu is one of the most notorious world leaders of the 21st century. This is true not only because he leads the small but well-known country of Israel, but also because he has frequently opposed world leaders to stand up for what he believes to be crucial and defining issues.

For example, he criticized U.S. President Barack Obama, in the White House, in front of cameras, for advocating a return to the 1967 borders. He challenged the West in opposing the nuclear deal that the world powers signed with Iran.

Many attempts have been made to understand what motivates Netanyahu to act in such a brash way. Some have simply dismissed him as an opportunistic politician more interested in his own political future than in the future of the free world. That assessment, however, would be unfair.

Netanyahu is one of the deepest thinkers among world leaders. As such, one should give him credit by trying to understand his worldview and assessing whether his actions make sense according to that worldview, before accusing him of opportunistic behavior.

Netanyahu comes from a very ideological family. His father, Benzion, sacrificed much for his ideology when he refused to align himself with David Ben-Gurion's Mapai Party, an act that cost him an academic career in Israel and forced him to move to America. Benjamin's brother Yoni was a famous national hero, who in combat and whose writings are still used to teach high-school students about Zionist values. This is not the type of background that creates opportunists.

To understand Netanyahu's philosophy, I believe that one must understand two complementary philosophies that form the backbone of his worldview: his father's deep skepticism on the one hand, and American conservative philosophy on the other.

Professor Benzion Netanyahu deeply influenced the prime minister's ethos. Prof. Netanyahu was a brilliant scholar of the Inquisition; he had been the secretary of Ze'ev Jabotinsky, the founder of Revisionist Zionism; and he was an emerging professional at the time of the Holocaust.

His academic focus as well as his first-hand experience of the Holocaust shaped his worldview, governed by a profoundly skeptical outlook.

Prof. Netanyahu theorized that Jewish suffering during the Spanish Inquisition was caused not only by anti-Semitic leaders but by the Jews' own utopian view of their situation. Their complacency blinded them to danger.

He described this as a form of Jewish self-deception.

In many ways, his arguments reveal an implicit criticism of the Jews who let their guard down many centuries later, as the Nazis rose to power.

This is what made Prof. Netanyahu identify with Jabotinsky's Revisionist Zionism, which later formed the basis for the Likud party. Revisionist Zionism did not speak of utopian dreams such as creating a "new Jew," or *tikkun olam*, but rather of making Jews stronger by teaching them to defend themselves as a nation.

This opposition to utopian ideals is what makes the prime minister such a strong realist, constantly arguing against the good intentions of his negotiating partners. It is also what makes Netanyahu so keen to focus on the defense requirements of the Jewish state when speaking of any agreement with the Palestinians.

He starts negotiating with the premise that his partner, whether a world leader or political opponent, is not to be trusted. And even if he could be trusted, who knows who would take his place in a few years? It is essential to move away from Jewish self-deception and not to let Israel's guard down.

This is also why the Iran deal worries Netanyahu. As long as an agreement is even partly dependent on the goodwill of the Iranian leaders—who continue to call for the destruction of the Jewish state and sponsor terrorist groups that attack Israel—Netanyahu views it as a deal with horrible consequences which must be opposed at all cost. Once again, the utopian ideology embraced by the Western world, led by President Barack Obama, who called for a "New Beginning" in the Middle East in the same way Shimon Peres once called for a "New Middle East," is for Netanyahu an existential threat to Israel.

However, this prudence and skepticism do not derive solely from the elder Netanyahu's philosophy.

Benjamin, who lived a significant part of his early life in the US, also has a deep connection to the American conservative political movement.

Conservative thinkers have often been reluctant to embrace the utopian views that progressives promulgate. As the world races forward without considering many of the sacrifices made in the name of "progress," the conservative asks of us to be prudent and not to make significant changes without serious thought.

William Buckley, founder of the National Review in 1955, an influential conservative thinker credited with reviving conservative thought in America, wrote in that magazine's mission statement that a conservative is someone who "stands athwart history, yelling Stop, at a time when no one is inclined to do so, or to have much patience with those who so urge it."

Is that not exactly the role that the prime minister has taken upon himself? While the world moved forward with a nuclear deal with Iran, and the U.S. administration implored detractors to have faith, Netanyahu—from the podium in the U.S. Congress—stood up and yelled "Stop!" This is not the first time he has done this.

During the Oslo Accords, as the world was mesmerized by the promise of utopian peace and a millennial almost-messianic fever with the end of war in sight (or the "End of History," to borrow Francis Fukuyama's phrase,), Netanyahu stood up said, "Stop!" when no one was willing to listen. It took only a few years for the world to see the true face of arch-terrorist Yasser Arafat and to understand that Netanyahu was right.

Today, even the Israeli Left has stopped talking about utopian peace agreements and speaks instead of unilateral withdrawals.

Netanyahu inherited a strong skepticism from his father and the motivation to prevent history's blunders from American conservatism. These two underlying forces explain why he takes a strong stand against what he views as a dangerous utopian vision of the world.

In fact, Obama himself accepts that this is the main difference between Netanyahu and himself. In an interview he gave to Israel's Channel 2, Obama tried to politely criticize Netanyahu. However, his criticism sounded more like a blessing to all those who embrace Netanyahu's prudent approach:

> We're always trying to balance a politics of hope and a politics of fear. And given the incredible tumult and chaos that's taking place in the Middle East, the hope of the Arab Spring that turned into the disasters of places like Syria, the rise of ISIL [Islamic State], the continuing expressions of anti-Semitism and anti-Israeli sentiment in so much of the Arab world, the rockets coming in from Gaza, the buildup of arms by Hezbollah—all those things, justifiably, make Israelis concerned about security, and security first.

Obama then continued:

> I think Prime Minister Netanyahu is somebody who's predisposed to think of security first; to think perhaps that peace is naïve; to see the worst possibilities as opposed to the best possibilities in Arab partners or Palestinian partners. And so I do think that, right now, those politics and those fears are driving the government's response. And I understand it. But my argument is that what may seem wise and prudent in the short term can actually end up being unwise over the long term.

The problem for Obama is that recent history has shown us that prudence is the right way, while utopian projects often end in disaster.

The very examples Obama brought up in that interview show how recent history seems to encourage us to embrace Netanyahu's worldview rather than his own. After all, Obama encouraged the Arab Spring, while Netanyahu expressed prudent concerns about it from the start.

The rise of the Islamic State and the current situation in Syria are a direct result of a policy embracing all progressive change without first thinking of the costs of those changes.

While Netanyahu might be criticized today for being the only voice opposing what many view as positive change, history has a habit of remembering those who stand up in the face of disastrous mistakes.

While we always hope that negative predictions turn out to be wrong, even when they are our own predictions, it is only logical to conclude that this is also how Netanyahu will be remembered.

ZIONISM AND NATIONALISM

Why You Should Be a Zionist

Ever since the U.N. General Assembly Resolution 3379 of 1975 declared "Zionism" a form of racism, the word has lost some of its public appeal.

The movement that represented a fight for freedom was rebranded as a movement of discrimination.

As the Boycott, Divestment, Sanctions (BDS) movement for the delegitimization of Israel gains ground and becomes a strategic threat, it has become important to go back to those very basic principles: the basic values that the Jewish state represents.

The principles outlined below have universal relevance. My claim is that Zionism is a movement that should inspire all people: both Jews and non-Jews.

There is a clear message here: The BDS movement is an enemy not only of Israel, but of all the universal values outlined below.

Zionism as a symbol of historical justice

The story of Zionism begins two thousand years ago, when the Jewish people were violently ejected from their homeland, the very area now called Israel. A yearning to return to their homeland would define them for the next two millenia.

S.Y. Agnon, Nobel Laureate in literature, put it best in his 1966 acceptance speech for that prize:

> As a result of the historic catastrophe in which Titus of Rome destroyed Jerusalem and Israel was exiled from its land, I was born in one of the cities of the exile. But always I regarded myself as one who was born in Jerusalem.

Prime Minister Benjamin Netanyahu expressed a similar historical outlook in a speech he gave to the U.S. Congress:

> In Judea and Samaria, the Jewish people are not foreign occupiers. We are not the British in India; we are not the Belgians in the Congo. This is the land of our forefathers, the Land of Israel, to which Abraham brought the idea of one God, where David set out to confront Goliath, and where Isaiah saw a vision of eternal peace. No distortion of history can deny the 4,000-year-old bond between the Jewish people and the Jewish land.

Two thousand years ago, the Jews were exiled from their land. The violent ethnic cleansing that took place so long ago might have been forgotten by history. However, history remembered the Jews, since the Jews never forgot their homeland. Almost two thousand years later, historic justice was achieved when the Jews returned to the Land of Israel and reestablished their own independent state.

The establishment of the State of Israel is nothing less than a symbol of historic justice. No amount of delegitimization, revisionist history or "alternative narratives" will change this plain fact.

Zionism as a symbol of positive nationalism

Nationalism has been given a negative reputation in the past few decades. The reason is obvious: Fascism is considered by many to be the ultimate form of nationalism.

After having witnessed the results of fascism, including Nazism, people reject anything relating to fascism.

However, true nationalism is not about hating others.

True nationalism is about loving your own.

Nationalism is not about negative feelings towards those who are different, but rather about a positive feeling of solidarity towards those who are members of your own nation. Just as a brother's love for his sister does not mean he must hate all others, so, too, the feeling of national solidarity should not be equated with negative feelings for others.

Zionism is deeply rooted in Jewish nationalism.

Jewish nationalism has its roots in the Hebrew Bible, in which God told Abraham: "And I will make you a great nation [...] And in you all the families of the earth will be blessed" (Genesis 2:2-3). This nationalism is, in its very essence, a positive nationalism. Yes, the Jewish nation is a distinct nation. However, the goal of this nation is to bring good to the world.

Since the establishment of the State of Israel, Jewish nationalism has contributed much to humanity. I am referring not only to the disproportionate number of Nobel laureates, or to the profusion of hi-tech innovation that has earned Israel the title, "Start-up Nation."

Whenever there is a humanitarian crisis caused by natural disasters, Israel is the first to respond. Israel's national army, the primary goal of which is to defend Israel, sees its role as defending other nations in crisis. One small example: Just a day following the devastating earthquake in Haiti in 2010, 220 Israelis were sent by Israel to help the victims, including teams of doctors and rescue and relief workers.

Israel sees its role as doing good to others.

Israel is a unique symbol of a truly positive nationalism.

Zionism as a symbol of freedom

While Jews yearned to go back to the Land of Israel for almost two thousand years, it never translated into political action. What happened in the late 18th century for Zionism to emerge as a political movement? With the rise of Western liberalism, the idea of freedom became central to the political discourse.

It was this political discourse which led Jews to seek freedom, as well. The "Jewish Enlightenment," which took place where they resided, was a first step. Across

Europe, individuals were granted liberties, and the Jews asked to receive those same rights.

Yet very quickly, it became clear that in order to get those rights, they would have to sacrifice their Jewishness: "Be a Jew inside your home, and a man on the street."

However, Judaism is not simply a religion that can be confined to one's home, but rather touches all aspects of one's life—including national, historical and cultural identity. It is impossible to be fully Jewish while keeping one's Jewishness "inside."

The Jewish people were divided between those who sought complete assimilation, and those who understood Zionism was the answer.

If Jews could not get their freedom in Europe, maybe the time had come to return to their historical homeland to obtain freedom? National freedom for the Jewish people, who had been under foreign rule for thousands of years, would provide the opportunity for individual freedom. Zionism was the movement for the freedom of the Jewish people, as well as the Jewish nation.

Of course, Zionism is not only a symbol for the national freedom of the Jewish nation. It has also, over time, become a symbol for individual freedom—in its ability to maximize individual freedoms given to ethnic and religious minorities, without sacrificing its national identity as the nation-state of the Jewish people.

Many theoretical academic books have been written analyzing the best ways to balance national identity with the rights of minorities. In many countries, these questions remain theoretical. In Israel, they are relevant every day. Israel has done a remarkable job of dealing with these complex issues.

Zionism as a symbol of democracy

Israel is also, of course, a democracy. Israel is the only stable democracy in the Middle East.

Looking at a map, Israel is geographically located on the front line of a battle between civilizations: those who embrace democracy, and those who do not.

This frontline is not only geographical but also ideological. Israel's enemies do not hide the fact that their enemy is the Western democratic world as a whole. Israel just happens to be the easiest target.

Democracy is more than simply a type of regime.

Democracy is a way to ensure that citizens participate in the system of government. The nation is not subservient to a ruler, but rather the ruler is subservient to the nation.

Almost no democracy has been able to stay as stable as Israel has been from its establishment. In America, when democracy was established, it was very limited, since it only represented the will of white males. In France, democracy did not survive very long, as Napoleon, who became a dictator, came on the heels of the Revolution.

There were many reasons to think that Israel would also fail in establishing a stable democracy. Many of its citizens came from countries (both eastern European and Arab countries) that did not have a democratic state or culture.

Also, war is a time in which even the most democratic countries temporarily put democratic principles on hold. Israel has been in a state of constant war since its establishment, and yet democracy has survived—even as the deep divisions within Israeli society could also fuel non-democratic behavior.

Zionism's astounding success in building a stable democracy makes it a symbol for democracy, not only in the Middle East, but throughout the world.

What do you oppose when opposing Zionism?

There are many more values for which Zionism serves as an ambassador. However, the above examples send a clear message: Those who support the BDS movement and oppose Zionism should know that when opposing Zionism, they are in fact opposing the principles of justice, freedom and democracy.

Their fight against Israel's right to exist is a fight for a world without these great values.

Those of us who believe in these values should join together and defend Israel against this new strategic threat.

The Case for Jewish Nationalism

The latest wave of attacks on Israelis by Palestinian terrorists brought in its wake a new surge in post-modernist moral relativism, bringing into question Israel's right to defend itself.

Such moral relativism is to be expected from the international media, as it is rooted in their misguided efforts to present a "balanced" portrayal of the conflict; although the moral principles of the two sides are not balanced. The correct response to the distortion that tries to make the Palestinian terrorists seem as moral as their Israeli victims, is to respond with facts that make the distorted picture clear again.

Unfortunately, moral relativism comes also from within Israel. Many of our media outlets have even questioned the morality of terrorist attacks on innocent civilians. Some Israeli journalists have asked government officials: "How else can an oppressed people respond to years of 'occupation?'" Others asked: "Why are police killing the perpetrators of the terrorist attacks instead of arresting them?" This ignores the fact that, in order to arrest a knife-yielding terrorist unafraid to die and intent on killing or maiming as many Israelis as possible, police officers would be endangering their own lives as well as others'.

Within Israel, questions like these should be seen as increasingly shocking, as they show a disintegration of our nationalist identity. National solidarity is being replaced by a post-modernist deconstruction of nationalism, pushing people towards misplaced criticism of their own nation rather than towards solidarity. This is how an Israeli policeman's blood becomes cheaper than a Palestinian terrorist's blood.

This disintegration comes from doubting the very nature of nationalism and patriotism in the light of universalistic and humanist values. It is time to reexamine the very nature of Jewish nationalism, as well as patriotism in general, in order to appreciate its critical value to humanity.

Nationalism is about love, not hate

The 20th century witnessed the most vicious forms of nationalism take root in some European countries, where it translated into fascism and even Nazism. This has made it easy for simplistic interpretations of the dangers of nationalism.

However, one should study its benefits before rejecting it.

Human relations are made of hierarchies.

For example, we feel a closer relationship to our own children than to other children, even than to our nephews.

The hierarchy continues; one feels a closer bond to a nephew than to the child of a complete stranger.

These hierarchies are a positive thing.

Could we imagine a world in which children were educated without the special passion of parental love? This hierarchy enhances bonds between people. Thus, close families are able to help each other when times get tough.

Together, families are stronger than just a collection of individuals.

A hierarchy does not in any way imply a negative feeling towards those on different levels. An increased love for one's child does not cause any level of hatred toward one's nephew. This was Plato's mistake in the Republic, in which he argued that a love for one's family would negatively impact patriotic feeling towards one's city. Plato tried to make familial ties at odds with the feeling of solidarity with one's city. His model never succeeded, since it not only opposed human nature, but also falsely assumed that increased solidarity for one group of people necessitated decreased solidarity for another.

Just as the hierarchy of human relations leads us to prefer immediate family to extended family, and extended family to strangers, patriotism guides us to prefer our own nation to another nation.

A preference for one's own nation does not translate into hatred or disdain for any other nation. Solidarity with one's own nation enables humanity to organize into groups of citizens to care for one another, help each other, and together define priorities to succeed as a group. The weak are cared for by the stronger, not because of coercive legislation, but out of a feeling of caring and solidarity.

This does not in any way impede the ability to help people of another nation.

Those who oppose nationalism based on humanist or universalistic grounds are no less misguided than Plato.

The Talmud, in the tractate *Bava Metzia*, shows that this hierarchical view is well entrenched in Jewish law and Jewish thought. Of charity, the Talmud says: "The poor of your city take precedence."

Just as this feeling of national solidarity is positive when it comes to charity, so too is it positive when it comes to defense. After all, one of the greatest manifestations of a father's love for his children is his willingness to do all that it takes in order to protect them. Thus, one should feel increased solidarity with one's compatriots when defending one's own nation from the attacks of other countries.

When the Israeli media take the side of the aggressor against the Israeli police or soldiers who are defending their people, this is not only a misunderstanding of the objective reality, it also wrongly justifies the aggressor while accusing the victim, demonstrating a disintegration of the essential and beneficial feeling of solidarity between the members of the Jewish nation.

The danger of nationalism

Even a great defender of the benefits of nationalism must also consider the dangers of nationalism.

After all, the 20th century gave us good reason to fear extreme forms of nationalism, in particular the rise of fascism in Europe. However, linking any form of national solidarity to fascism is like linking regular healthy eating to the feasts on which Roman emperors gorged themselves. Nationalism can be positive, but history has shown extreme forms of it to be extremely negative.

The problem with fascism is twofold.

On an internal level, fascism's complete disregard for individual freedom made nationalism a tool for dictators rather than a tool for healthy national solidarity. True nationalism does not need to come with a coercive government. True nationalism actually warrants a "laissez-faire" approach, since solidarity between people makes government intervention less necessary.

On an external level, fascism linked a feeling of national solidarity with a disregard for other people's rights. This is not the positive nationalism that we have described, which combines national solidarity with general solidarity between all of humanity. It would be a mistake to let the fear of fascism make us overlook the essential benefits of nationalism.

The case of Jewish nationalism

In the specific case of Jewish nationalism, there is less fear of slipping into fascism.

Jewish nationalism is based on Jewish philosophy, which calls on Israel to become a light unto the nations, a nation that exists for the purpose of doing good for the whole world. A nation with such a mission statement can hardly misinterpret national solidarity with hatred towards other nations. This would contradict the mission statement completely.

In this post-modern age, as people question and deconstruct basic principles of human nature, human interactions and society, one must be careful to prevent the dismantlement of social constructs that provide humanity with many positive aspects. Nationalism, and national solidarity, is one of those constructs that should not be discarded.

Academics debate whether nationalism is essential to human nature or whether it is a social construct created by humans, but this academic discussion is moot. The basic fact is that nationalism provides positive benefits to human society, and, as such, it must be preserved. This is true whether nationalism is man-made or whether it is innate to human nature, and it is all the more applicable when talking about Jewish nationalism.

Bernie Sanders, Anti-Semites and American Jewish Identity

Bernie Sanders is the only Jew to have ever come so far in an American presidential primary, challenging Hillary Clinton for the Democratic nomination right to the end of the 2016 primary season. He is the Jew who has come closest to being President of the United States. Even if he did not win the democratic nomination, this is still a historical achievement.

As such, many have frowned at the fact that the Sanders campaign has failed to properly highlight this historic moment. In fact, Sanders seemed intent on hiding that he is Jewish so as not to hurt his chances of winning the nomination.

In a debate in March 2016, Sanders was asked point blank why he never mentioned his Jewish identity. His unfortunate answer makes us wonder whether it would not have been better for Sanders not to answer at all.

Anderson Cooper asked Sanders: "Just this weekend there was an article I read in the Detroit News saying that you keep your Judaism in the background, and that's disappointing some Jewish leaders. Is that intentional?"

In response, Sanders answered: "No. I am very proud to be Jewish, and being Jewish is so much of what I am."

If he would have stopped there, Sanders' answer would have made most Jews content and proud. After all, we have a viable candidate for the role of leader of the free world proudly proclaiming his pride in his Jewish heritage!

However, Sanders went on to qualify his statement by explaining why he was proud to be Jewish, and thus giving us a look into the foundation of his Jewish identity.

Sanders said: "Look, my father's family was wiped out by Hitler in the Holocaust. I know about what crazy and radical, and extremist politics mean. I learned that lesson as a tiny, tiny child when my mother would take me shopping, and we would see people working in stores who had numbers on their arms because they were in Hitler's concentration camp."

This is Sanders' Jewish identity. It is an identity based not on Judaism but on anti-Semitism. It is an identity which ignores the accomplishments of the Jewish people and bases itself on remembering the accomplishments of the Jewish nation's worst enemies. The anti-Semites define what Judaism is for Sanders.

Of course, no one should minimize the importance of remembering the Holocaust. It is a defining moment of Jewish history, and the Jewish world is much better off remembering it than forgetting it. Moreover, if we want to ensure that the Holocaust will never be repeated— neither to Jews nor to any other people—we must remember. We must never forget.

However, as important as remembrance is, it should never supersede our Jewish identity. It must never become the defining factor of our Jewishness.

Why did Sanders not mention with great pride that he is the son of Abraham, the patriarch of the Jewish nation who fought against the violent paganism and brought about the morality of monotheism to this world?

Why did Sanders not mention Moses who led the Jews out of Egypt, in the first instance of history where slaves were freed from bondage, an instance which has remained an inspiration for all movements for freedom and liberty up until this very day?

How could Sanders forget King David and his inspiring poetry, as collected in psalms, and speak with pride of the leader of the Jewish nation that was at once a great artist and a great military strategist.

Did Sanders not know about the Hasmoneans or the Bar Kochba revolt, two instances in which the Jewish nation fought bravely against global empires in order to protect their right to the free practice of religion and against religious discrimination?

How could Sanders not have mentioned the Talmud, one of the greatest collections of wisdom ever written, which is still studies on a daily basis by such a large part of the Jewish nation?

Why did Sanders not mention Maimonides or Rabbi Judah Halevy, two medieval Jewish philosophers who remain some of the greatest philosophers in history?

How could Sanders not even mention Spinoza, Marx, Freud or Einstein, who each broke the frontiers of their disciplines, for better or worse, but always pushing further and reaching new heights?

Most importantly, how could Sanders ignore Herzl, Jabotinsky, Ben Gurion and Begin, the founding fathers of the state of Israel, or Yoni Netanyahu, Roee Klein, and all the other modern day heroes risking their lives in the IDF in the fight against terrorism. How could he ignore the great Hebrew poets of the past century, from Hayim Nahman Bialik and Naomi Shemer to Rabbi David Buzaglo, who helped revive the Hebrew language that was once dead? How could he ignore the fact that we live in an age where the Jewish people have returned to their land after two thousand years of exile, coming home from Morocco to Iran and France, Yemen, Poland, Ethiopia and Russia, the only nation to ever accomplish such an unlikely accomplishment.

How can Sanders reduce such an incredible history to the horrible events of the Holocaust? Is that really the most defining feature of Jewish history?

In fact, Sanders' simplistic rendering of his relationship to Judaism reflects a problem with Jewish identity within the American Jewish world. In a widely published PEW research report from 2013, when asked what it means to be Jewish, 73% of respondents answered that remembering the Holocaust is an essential part of what being Jewish means to them. This was the most widely expressed opinion. By comparison, only 43% claimed that caring about Israel was essential and only 19% believed that Jewish Law was an essential part of their Jewish identity. Only one of the eight other options, "leading an ethical life," ranked almost as highly (69%) as "remembering the Holocaust."

If American Jewish identity consists primarily of remembering only the worst parts of recent Jewish history, while we are living in one of the most incredible periods of Jewish history, is it any surprise that many Jews are leaving the Jewish tradition and assimilating into American society? Is there anyone who wants to be a victim? It is therefore no surprise that this same study shows the intermarriage rate is at 58%, up from 43% in 1990 and 17% in 1970.

Charles Krauthammer, an American Jewish political commentator, recently quoted Emil Fackenheim, a Jewish philosopher, to explain that, if there are 613 commandments in traditional Judaism, the 614th is to deny Hitler any posthumous victories. Krauthammer went on to say that "the reduction of Jewish identity to victimhood would be one such victory. It must not be permitted." We should never allow the anti-Semites to define who we are.

With such an extraordinary history, of which the Jewish people can be proud, it is beyond comprehension as to why the primary focus of American Jewish identity would remain victimhood rather than intense pride in one's heritage.

Jewish communities and educators should aim to broaden the knowledge and connection of American Jews to all aspects of Jewish culture, including the Holocaust but not limiting it to this or similar anti-Semitic events, so that they can see that they have much to be proud of. If this heritage were presented to them more frequently, they would, without a doubt, embrace it much more than the victimhood-based version of Judaism. This is the great challenge of Jewish educators in the United States.

A Critique of Palestinian Nationalism

One of the Zionist Left's strongest arguments is based on the very principles that lie at the foundation of Zionist nationalism and the right to self-determination.

The Zionist Left argues that Zionism doesn't simply allow for the creation of a Palestinian state, it mandates it.

How so? If Zionism is based on the universal belief in the righteousness of nationalism and in the right to the self-determination of all nations, including the Jewish nation, how can a true Zionist be opposed to this when it comes to the Palestinian people? This argument is quite convincing, especially to all those who seek in Zionism some universal values that transcend the traditional Jewish attachment to the Land of Israel.

However, this argument is also based on some flawed assumptions that need to be deconstructed.

Are the Palestinians really a nation?

Historically, the idea of a Palestinian nation is very new.

For some time, Palestine was merely a geographical area—not a national identity. There were Palestinian

Arabs, Palestinian Beduin and Palestinian Jews. These terms simply referred to Arabs, Beduin or Jews living in the geographical region of Palestine.

James L. Gelvin writes in his book *The Israel-Palestine Conflict: One Hundred Years of War.* "Palestinian nationalism emerged during the inter-war period, in response to Zionist immigration and settlement." In fact, the mufti of Jerusalem, Haj Amin al-Husseini, who had ties to Nazi Germany, deliberately cultivated Palestinian nationalism.

As historian Bernard Lewis postulates: "The rewriting of the past is usually undertaken to achieve specific political aims."

One argument is that the history of Palestinian nationalism is not very important; if Palestinian nationalism exists today, then that is what matters.

This would be true if we did not have modern evidence of Palestinians self-identifying not as a separate nation, but as part of the Arab nation as a whole, rejecting the idea of Palestinian nationalism.

Indeed, on March 31, 1977, Dutch newspaper Trouw published an interview with PLO executive committee member Zahir Muhsein, in which he said: "The Palestinian people does not exist. The creation of a Palestinian state is only a means for continuing our struggle against the State of Israel for our Arab unity. In reality, today there is no difference between Jordanians, Palestinians, Syrians and Lebanese. Only for political and tactical reasons do we speak today about the existence of a Palestinian people, since Arab national interests demand that we posit the existence of a distinct 'Palestinian people' to oppose Zionism."

Even the Palestinian National Charter's Article 1 is clear: "The Palestinian people are an integral part of the Arab nation."

Moreover, Balad Party founder Azmi Bishara, an Israeli Arab, stated in an interview: "Well, I don't think there is a Palestinian nation at all; I think there is an Arab nation. I always thought so, and I have not changed my mind."

Are all nations entitled to a state?

Even if we were to take as a basic assumption that the Palestinian nation were real, and if we were to give every group of people the right to spontaneously declare themselves a nation, does this mean that all nations have a right to statehood? To answer this, we should first look at the context in which this question is being asked— among numerous groups with a much more convincing claim to nationhood but are nevertheless deprived of their right to a state. The Kurds are the clearest example of this but we can list dozens others, from the Québécois in Canada, through the Catalan people in Spain, to the Kabyle in Algeria and of course the Tibetan people in China. The globe is filled with stateless nations!

Still, while this context clearly begs the question as to why the world is so obsessed with the claims of Palestinians for statehood, an injustice against a third party does not justify an injustice performed against a group of people.

However, here one must ask: What exactly is the right to self-determination that nations enjoy? Must it take the form of an official state, or can it be actualized via other means, such as political autonomy? Today, the Palestinians choose their own leaders.

They have their own parliament, government and police force. They do not have control over immigration, and they do not have an army. Borders and the military are what differentiates them from a regular state, and the reasons why Israel refuses to grant the Palestinians control over their borders and military are totally justified. Granting them these concessions would endanger Israel's very existence.

Can Palestinians really claim that their basic right to self-determination is being hindered when they are already ruling themselves? Does self-determination take precedence over all other rights? Any rights discourse always comes down to a balance between the rights of the different parties.

Therefore, even if we were to (falsely) assume that Palestinian nationalism were real, and even if we were to (falsely) assume that Palestinian nationalism meant a right to a full Palestinian state, we would still have to balance these rights with the other side's claims.

Israel has very strong claims to the Land of Israel, including Judea and Samaria. These claims exist on many levels: a strong legal case, based on international law as defined in the British Mandate, which convincingly and beyond any reasonable doubt defined Israel as a Jewish state; a strong historical case dating back several millennia that shows the striking connection of the Jewish people to these areas, which were the beacon of Jewish civilization; and a clear security argument that justifies limiting the rights of Israel's sworn enemies, which call for its destruction.

All of these claims together must be balanced with the Palestinians' clamoring for self-determination.

In such a scenario, is it not justified to say these claims should be exercised not through a state but through an autonomous government, in the way they exercise it today?

Should we support all types of nationalism?

Finally, in order to properly assess this crucial question, we must take a step back and ask: What does Palestinian nationalism stand for? What is the essence of Palestinian nationalism? Are we to support any type of nationalism, even if negative? Jewish nationalism stands for the Jewish values of loving your neighbor as yourself, love for your land, and believing in building a nation which will become a light unto the nations. American nationalism stands for freedom. French nationalism stands for liberty, equality and brotherhood.

What does Palestinian nationalism stand for?

In order to understand this, we need to ask: What makes Palestinian nationalism unique when compared to the brotherly manifestation of Arab nationalism? This uniqueness is the essence of Palestinian nationalism.

Scrutiny of Palestinian nationalism quickly reveals that it stands for one thing, and one thing only—the denial of Jewish nationalism. One small example: If we look at the Palestinian national holiday, we find two main ones. The *Nakba* is the day when Palestinians mourn the establishment of the State of Israel, and the *Naksa* is the day when Palestinians mourn the liberation of Jerusalem by Israel.

In other words, supporting Palestinian nationalism as a concept is opposing Jewish nationalism.

It denies Israel's right to exist. Palestinian nationalism is not a movement worth supporting—it should be opposed.

The bottom line: Jewish nationalism cannot be compared to Palestinian nationalism.

When left-wing Zionists compare Jewish nationalism to Palestinian nationalism, they are comparing the incomparable.

Jewish nationalism has existed for thousands of years; it is older than most other forms of nationalism, and it is based on the positive values of love: for one's nation, for one's land and for a better world.

Palestinian nationalism is a recent invention.

It is not even clear if it exists today, based on the declarations of the Palestinians themselves. It is also a movement based on negative values: denying the right of others to exist.

The comparison between the movements is nothing less than a cynical blasphemy.

If, to the Zionist Left, Jewish nationalism is not more valuable than Palestinian nationalism, then one must question how much left-wing Zionists truly value Zionism.

FOREIGN POLICY
AND SECURITY

The Shattering of Western Myths by the Islamic State

Many people were shocked when they first heard of the Islamic State (IS), a small terrorist group that took over large parts of Iraq and Syria and declared itself a new caliphate in June 2014. The rise of IS-inspired terrorist activity across Europe, North America and Australia has only enhanced this shock.

However, those who heeded the constant warnings coming from Israel about the dangers of the Middle East have anticipated such an event for a long time.

In this section, I want to examine the various lessons that the rise of IS can teach us about the Middle East. One can quickly discern that these are exactly the things Israel has been talking about for the past few decades, shattering many Western myths.

1. The Israeli-Palestinian conflict is not the central conflict in the Middle East.

For the past few decades, the Western world has acted as if the root of all problems in the Middle East is the Israeli-Palestinian conflict. If only we could solve this one problem, it thought, we could bring about peace in the Middle East.

The events of the past few years prove that the problems in the Middle East are much deeper than the one conflict between the Jewish state and the Arab world.

The struggle between Sunnis and Shi'ites far predates the struggle between the Arab world and Israel. It is specifically this struggle that is at the heart of the battle between IS and the government forces in Iraq. The struggle between secular and religious forces lies at the heart of many of the conflicts in the region, including the conflict between the Muslim Brotherhood and the Egyptian government, and the internal conflict in Syria. There is also an age-old battle with various groups in the region trying to gain some form of autonomy, or at least some equal rights: the Kurds, the Alawites, the Yazidis, the Druze and the Christians.

These historical conflicts, some dating back over 1,000 years, are much deeper than the Jewish-Arab one. These conflicts were silenced by strong dictatorships in the region that silenced any opposition. However, with the advent of the Arab Spring and the weakening of these dictatorships, these conflicts are now reviving.

In just the past few years, hundreds of thousands have died in these conflicts—many more deaths than have resulted from the Israeli-Palestinian conflict.

Let us put what is already clear even more bluntly: The building of Jewish houses in the Jewish historical homeland of Judea and Samaria, in Israel, has absolutely nothing to do with these conflicts, and no peace deal between Palestinians and Jews could ever help solve them.

2. Territorial withdrawals strengthen terrorism.

For the past few decades, many analysts have claimed that territorial depth has stopped being an important factor in wars, which have become far more technological in nature. This means that territorial withdrawals should not be feared, since technology could compensate for the loss of control over territory.

However, recent experience shows that there is no substitute for actual control over a territory.

The United States completed its withdrawal from Iraq on December 18, 2011.

By June 2014, IS had already taken over large swathes of Iraq, and the Iraqi government was left defenseless. The vacuum left by the withdrawal of a Western army from a territory leads to chaos, encouraging extremist elements to take over. This is also what happened after Israel withdrew from Gaza in August 2005, with Hamas taking over in January 2006. When Western democracies leave behind a territory without proper preparation and stability, terrorists take over.

In the 2008 elections, the Obama administration ridiculed presidential candidate John McCain for claiming that US troops might have to stay in Iraq for over 100 years. McCain claimed that the troops had to stay "as long as it takes," even if it was in smaller numbers. He gave examples of other conflicts in which American troops stayed for decades as passive forces to ensure stability.

He said:

> If we had withdrawn six months ago, I can look you in the eye and tell you that al-Qaida would have said, 'We beat the United States of America.' If we'd gone along with Harry Reid and said the war is lost to al-Qaida, then we would be fighting that battle all over the Middle East.

Barack Obama won the presidential election, as the Iraq war was incredibly unpopular then. However, looking back, it is clear that McCain was right, and that Obama is the one who should have been ridiculed for his rushed judgment and his lack of understanding of the region. As soon as America left Iraq, Islamists gained in strength and slowly took over.

Yes, Obama's rash judgment was what led to the rushed withdrawal of troops, to the strengthening of IS and to all the horrors that have now landed on our television screens: genocide, beheadings, mass graves and more.

On August 8, 2014, Obama, the greatest advocate of territorial withdrawal, announced that he had authorized an air strike in Iraq. Even the one of the most non-interventionist presidents in recent history was forced to intervene in Iraq to deal with the chaos that ensued following the withdrawal of American troops.

It should come as no surprise that Israel, too, nine years after the unilateral withdrawal from Gaza, went back into Gaza in Operation Protective Edge, defending itself against rocket attacks from a vicious terrorist organization whose stated goal is to kill as many Israeli citizens as possible.

Territorial withdrawals are dangerous.

Those done without proper preparation lead to disaster. They strengthen extremist organizations that thrive in chaotic situations and give them an opportunity to take control.

3. Iran needs to be stopped.

As we witness IS's violence, we must remember that there are few tactical differences between Islamic State and the Islamic Republic of Iran. Both are governed by radical Islam. Both want to apply Shari'a law in their territories and are regularly violate human-rights. Both have expansionist agendas—Islamic State through traditional expansion, Iran via proxies such as Hezbollah.

The only reason for conflict between Iran and IS is that one is Shi'ite and the other is Sunni.

Giving Iran the capability for producing a nuclear bomb is exactly like handing a nuclear bomb to IS. This is an existential threat not only to Israel, but for the whole world. It must be stopped.

4. Israel must stand up to pressure.

As recent events have shown, utopian experts from around the world who have pressured Israel have now been proven wrong.

It is Israel that has been proven right, with its reticence to leave territory that is under its control, its insistence that Israel is not the root cause of the troubles in the Middle East, and its call for the international community to ensure that Iran never gets a nuclear weapon.

Instead of pressuring Israel, the world should start listening to Israel. Until then, Israel must stand up to international pressure.

Defeating Neo-Terrorism

A new form of terrorism is ravaging Israel. Gone are the days when terrorist groups such as Hamas, Fatah or the Islamic Jihad would train recruits, provide them with weapons and send them on missions. Instead, neo-terrorism is about individuals independently planning and implementing a terrorist attack.

Traditional terrorism could be combated by dismantling the network necessary for these attacks to take place, but neo-terrorism does not need such a network. All that is needed is an individual with a car or a knife and a will to kill.

If traditional terrorism involved long periods of planning for each attack and a number of different people involved in this planning, all of which enabled the intelligence community to intercept these planned attacks, then neo-terrorism is planned and executed by one individual who spontaneously decides the time has come to kill Jews.

The role of the terrorist organization has shifted from planning the attacks to using new media to incite individuals to commit terrorist acts. The rise in popularity of Islamic State only adds fuel to this fire and encourages radical Islamists to act on their beliefs.

The old strategies for combating traditional terrorism are not working anymore. As Israelis ask for solutions to the current wave of terrorist attacks, the number of these attacks keeps rising.

No solution is in sight. Israelis grow more and more frustrated by government inaction, while government officials, in private conversations, are admitting that they do not have a real strategy to deal with this form of terrorism.

Shifting our focus to the goals of the terrorists

It is time to shift our way of thinking.

Previously, Israel used intelligence as a means of preventing terrorists from planning and executing attacks. While this strategy should still be used to ensure that traditional terrorism will not resurface, it is not helpful in fighting neo-terrorism.

To fight neo-terrorism, Israel needs to shift its focus from an intelligence-based strategy to a psychological-analysis based strategy.

First, Israel must ask itself: What are the terrorists trying to accomplish with each attack? What are their goals? What would they consider a successful outcome of a terrorist attack? Then, based on this psychological analysis, the Israel's response to each terrorist attack must ensure that, at the very least, the attacks do not achieve these goals. When possible, Israel should even make sure that these attacks should be counterproductive and bring about opposite results than those hoped for by the terrorist.

For example, the stated purpose of the latest wave of terrorist attacks has been the protection of al-Aksa Mosque and the Dome of the Rock on the Temple Mount that the Palestinians falsely claim the Jews are trying to destroy.

If the purpose of the terrorist attacks is to ensure Muslim control over the Temple Mount, then every time a terrorist attack occurs, the Temple Mount should be closed for 24 hours to Muslims, as it is so often closed to Jews wishing to visit the holiest site of Judaism. At first thought, this might sound like a recipe for escalation.

However, if it becomes clear that every escalation will only hurt Muslim worship on the Temple Mount, the result will be that the terrorists will finally understand that violence and terrorism are not tools with which they will reach their goals.

The goals of neo-terrorism

While the stated goal of this new wave of terrorism, as mentioned, is the protection of the Temple Mount, there are additional reasons for it.

Of course, terrorism has been used as a way to scare Jews into leaving the parts of Israel that it liberated in 1967. The perpetrators hope that as terrorism becomes more common, Jews will retreat and admit defeat. This would be, in their minds, the first step to the demise of the State of Israel.

If terrorists are trying to make Israel move back its borders, then the way to fight terrorism is to make every terrorist attack a reason for deepening our ties with the disputed territories.

Every terrorist attack should be translated into the establishment of a new city in Judea and Samaria.

Very quickly, the terrorists will understand that instead of making Israel retreat, their attacks are counterproductive and make any hope for Israeli retreat much less likely.

Instead of bringing about the destruction of Israel, each terrorist attack should bring about further building of Israel. Every victim should see a city rise in his name.

Another goal of neo-terrorism is to protest the treatment of the Palestinians in the disputed territories. People who feel oppressed use violence to battle their perceived oppressors.

While every society has its faults, and Israel can definitely improve some specific aspects of its treatment of Palestinians, it can in no way accept this as a result of neo-terrorism.

Rather, the opposite must happen. Every time a terrorist strikes at Israel, Palestinians must feel their standard of living go down.

First of all, the Israeli government must destroy the house of the attacker to make sure his immediate family's standard of living will never be the same. Then, Israel must send massive troops to the villages in the area that the terrorist comes from to show a clear presence.

Potential terrorists need to see that terrorism does not lead to a better standard of living for their fellow Palestinians. They need to understand that terrorism will only worsen the conditions in which their fellow Palestinians are living.

Setting a new standard

For this new strategy to be effective, it has to become the new standard.

Israel has to set clear rules as to the repercussions of terrorist attacks, and it needs to abide by these rules religiously, without thinking twice and without hesitation.

When the automatic consequence of a terrorist attack includes things such as the closing of the Temple Mount to Muslim prayer, the building of a new city in Judea and Samaria and the destruction of the terrorists' homes, individuals incited to wake up one day and commit a spontaneous terrorist attack will understand that these attacks will not only be unproductive, they will be counterproductive.

Only then will we see a decline in the number of terrorist attacks in Israel.

Building a new iron wall

In 1923, Ze'ev Jabotinsky wrote an essay, "The Iron Wall," which has become the foundation of Israel's defense strategy. In it, Jabotinsky argued at length that it would be impossible to convince the Arabs to agree willingly to the establishment of a Jewish state in Israel.

He then came to the conclusion that the only way for Arabs to stop attacking the Jews in Israel is for them to understand that the Jewish presence in Israel is here to stay, strong like an iron wall, and that their attacks are not productive. Only then will they leave their extremist ways and approach Israel's existence with more moderately.

Jabotinsky's worldview served as the basis for the establishment of the Hagana and the defense methodology in the Jewish settlements before the establishment of the State of Israel. It was then translated into the defense strategy of Israel's army by prime minister David Ben-Gurion, who understood that Israel could not destroy more than five Arab armies, but that Israel should focus instead on making it clear to these armies that they could also not defeat Israel militarily, as it will stand strong forever like an iron wall.

Neo-terrorism warrants a new translation and application of those same principles. Israel cannot use intelligence as a means of stopping every individual with a car or knife from committing a terrorist attack.

However, Israel can make it clear that the terrorists' goals will never be furthered through violent means. Israel can make sure that terrorists realize that these attacks will only be counterproductive.

Only then will neo-terrorism be defeated, the way Jabotinsky's strategy defeated pre-state violence and the way Ben-Gurion's strategy convinced the Arab armies to stop attacking Israel.

Bin Laden's Victory over Obama's America

Osama bin Laden was killed by American forces on May 2, 2011. This event was, without a doubt, a physical victory for America over al-Qaida.

However, an analysis of America's strategic shift with respect to foreign policy will show that when it comes to the broader strategic war of civilizations, bin Laden himself had a decisive victory.

In a famous open letter to the American people in November, 2002, bin Laden explained his motivation for attacking America and the changes that he demanded be implemented before he would refrain from attacking the country.

These changes include some ridiculous demands such as mass conversion to Islam, but we will limit our analysis to the actual strategic demands bin Laden made of America. We will then see how U.S. President Barack Obama's administration worked to implement every single one of these demands.

Retreat of American forces from Muslim lands

One of the demands was for the immediate retreat of American troops from Muslim lands: "Your forces occupy our countries; you spread your military bases throughout them; you corrupt our lands, and you besiege our sanctities," bin Laden argued. "We also advise you to pack your luggage and get out of our lands. We desire for your goodness, guidance and righteousness, so do not force us to send you back as cargo in coffins."

One of the main issues to come up in the 2008 election was the question of the presence of American troops in Iraq. Republican candidate John McCain argued that troops should be left for as long as needed in order to provide stability, "maybe even 100 years." Obama, on the other hand, promised immediate withdrawal. Obama won the election and began the withdrawal of troops from the Middle East in 2009, completing it by 2011. Of course, this withdrawal created the vacuum needed for ISIS to emerge; however, this will be the subject of other chapters in this book. The fact is that Obama withdrew troops in just the way Bin Laden had hoped.

In June, 2011, Obama announced a change in strategy in Afghanistan, calling for the "drawdown" of troops at a steady pace. The plan called for the complete withdrawal of combat troops by the end of 2014. "The tide of war is receding," he said.

The military argued for maintaining a more significant presence, while the Obama administration wanted a very small presence. As a result of increasingly frustrating dealings with President Hamid Karzai, Obama was even giving serious consideration in early July, 2013 to speeding up the withdrawal of forces, and to a "zero option" that would leave no American troops there after 2014.

After 13 years, Britain, the United States and the remaining Australians officially ended their combat operations in Afghanistan on October 28, 2014 with only minor forces left behind, primarily intended to train Afghan forces. Yet at the end of March, 2015, U.S. President Obama announced slowing the pace of the U.S. troop withdrawal by maintaining the 2016 force levels of 9,800 troops. Still, even if the reality on the ground does not permit a full withdrawal, it is clear that this Obama's wish.

Bin Laden's legacy lives on.

Non-intervention as foreign policy

Bin Laden's other strategic demand in his letter was for America to stop meddling in the business of other countries: "We call upon you to end your support of the corrupt leaders in our countries. Do not interfere in our politics and method of education. Leave us alone, or else expect us in New York and Washington."

The Obama administration made this its strategic plan. On the one hand, Obama stopped supporting strategic allies, such as Hosni Mubarak. When the people of Egypt rose against him, Obama pressured him to resign.

On the other hand, Obama stopped showing strong opposition to America's enemies. While clearly stating that any use of chemical weapons by Syria would be a redline that would force American intervention in the conflict, when President Bashar Assad used chemical weapons, Obama did not intervene—and Assad still rules, at the time of this publication, over Syria.

Iran is no longer treated like a real enemy. Sanctions have been lifted; a deal has been signed; there have even been photo shoots of John Kerry and Iranian Foreign Minister Mohammad Javad Zarif. What has Tehran given up to deserve this treatment? Nothing substantial. Iran still calls for the destruction of Israel; it still reserves the right to nuclear technology in the future.

With America's enemies receiving such treatment, Mubarak probably wished he had been considered an enemy rather than a friend. In fact, there is clear incentive nowadays for US allies to look for other allies, rather than to rely on American support.

This new strategy of non-intervention is the complete opposite of the American foreign relations strategy that bin Laden opposed.

Before bin Laden's victory over the American spirit, the US saw itself as a moral beacon in the world, a messenger of freedom and liberty; part of the American mission was to spread this liberty. This bothered bin Laden, since his message was one of submission to Islam and support of dictatorships, not freedom.

Now, while America has of course not submitted itself to Islam, it has clearly shown that it is not bothered when others are forcefully coerced into submitting to it. America is also not bothered by tyrants and dictatorship. All that matters is that America cannot be bothered. "Leave us alone in New York and Washington, and we will not interfere in your affairs"—this is the new American message.

America went from being leader of the free world, bringing good, to being just another country.

Stop supporting Israel

Of course, one of bin Laden's central demands was for America to stop supporting Israel: "Palestine, which has sunk under military occupation for more than 80 years...The British handed over Palestine, with your help and your support, to the Jews, who have occupied it for more than 50 years; years overflowing with oppression, tyranny, crimes, killing, expulsion, destruction and devastation. The creation and continuation of Israel is one of the greatest crimes, and you are the leaders of its criminals. And of course there is no need to explain and prove the degree of American support for Israel."

He added: "We also advise you to stop supporting Israel."

It would be an exaggeration to claim that bin Laden's victory on this subject has been complete. After all, his claim was that the occupation by "Jews" in "Palestine" started over 50 years ago. In other words, he is opposed to the very existence of Israel.

However, there is no doubt that on this issue as well, bin Laden did score some valuable points.

In 2010, U.S. Vice President Joe Biden spoke in very clear terms: "There is absolutely no space between the US and Israel—none, none at all."

In private conversations, however, the tone was very different. This is clear from a private meeting between Obama and Malcolm Hoenlein, executive vice chairman

America went from being leader of the free world, bringing good, to being just another country.

Stop supporting Israel

Of course, one of bin Laden's central demands was for America to stop supporting Israel: "Palestine, which has sunk under military occupation for more than 80 years ... The British handed over Palestine, with your help and your support, to the Jews, who have occupied it for more than 50 years; years overflowing with oppression, tyranny, crimes, killing, expulsion, destruction and devastation. The creation and continuation of Israel is one of the greatest crimes, and you are the leaders of its criminals. And of course there is no need to explain and prove the degree of American support for Israel."

He added: "We also advise you to stop supporting Israel."

It would be an exaggeration to claim that bin Laden's victory on this subject has been complete. After all, his claim was that the occupation by "Jews" in "Palestine" started over 50 years ago. In other words, he is opposed to the very existence of Israel.

However, there is no doubt that on this issue as well, bin Laden did score some valuable points.

In 2010, U.S. Vice President Joe Biden spoke in very clear terms: "There is absolutely no space between the US and Israel—none, none at all."

In private conversations, however, the tone was very different. This is clear from a private meeting between Obama and Malcolm Hoenlein, executive vice chairman of the Conference of Presidents of Major American Jewish Organizations: "If you want Israel to take risks, then its leaders must know that the US is right next to them," Hoenlein told the president.

Obama disagreed.

"Look at the past eight years," he said, referring to the George W. Bush administration. "During those eight years, there was no space between us and Israel, and what did we get from that? When there is no daylight, Israel just sits on the sidelines, and that erodes our credibility with the Arab states."

During Obama's term, led by Secretary of State John Kerry, America has made it clear to the world that there is a lot of daylight between the two countries. Kerry pressures Prime Minister Benjamin Netanyahu to make more and more concessions, even after Netanyahu endorsed the two-state solution, had a settlement frozen and released violent murderers from Israeli prisons.

At the same time, he has not asked for any concessions from Palestinian Authority President Mahmoud Abbas, who has still not recognized Israel's basic right to exist as the nation-state of the Jewish people.

In effect, Netanyahu keeps moving towards Obama and Obama keeps taking a step back towards Abbas, keeping a lot of daylight between the two countries.

Yes, America still recognizes Israel's right to exist, but America is not Israel's closest ally. Bin Laden is probably smiling in his nonexistent grave for this additional victory.

Leader of the free world?

The Obama administration has taken a clear stand against being the leader of the free world. In doing so, it has clearly submitted a large part of its worldview to that of bin Laden.

Those of us who cherish freedom and want its success, and who believe in America's contribution to the world, should urge the American people to ensure the next administration reverses this strategic shift. Then, America will be able to declare victory not only against bin Laden's physical body, but also against his legacy.

Why does Israel keep losing the public diplomacy battle?

As Israel's image in the world keeps deteriorating, her supporters need to start using innovative methods to promote the nation's positive image.

Israel's international image has taken a severe blow in the past few years. With numerous and continuous public diplomacy crises, Israel's advocates worldwide must be starting to ask themselves what they are doing wrong. If failures steadily occur, there must be something wrong with the actual base strategy we are using—and we must change it.

Let us first look at some of the recent failures in public diplomacy: firstly, the BDS movement.

Working since 2005 to boycott, divest and implement sanctions against Israel, the movement has recently gained strength, and has successfully convinced artists and public figures to join in their boycott of Israel. Their latest supporter was none other than celebrated physicist Stephen Hawking.

The flotilla incident is also still being interpreted by many as an aggression on Israel's part, even after the Israeli advocacy community has quite convincingly demonstrated that the soldiers acted in self-defense.

Arrest warrants have been issued for even some of the most dovish politicians, such as Tzipi Livni, who refrained from visiting London in 2009 after a UK court issued an arrest warrant.

Israel keeps getting accused of war crimes and massacres. Protests against Israel are taking place all around the world, and human rights groups regularly criticize the Jewish state. Several initiatives attempting to mark and eventual boycott settlement goods are rapidly gaining ground in Europe.

The failures of Israel's public diplomacy can best be summarized by looking at the Global Peace Index, an annual peacefulness ranking of the world's nations. Israel has continuously dropped in the rankings. In 2012, Israel was considered less peaceful than countries such as Syria and Libya.

As a Zionist who understands Israel's cause and its positive influence on this world, my first reaction when thinking about all of these failures is frustration, followed by an attempt to blame the natural bias that the world seems to have against the Jewish state. However, those of us who aren't content to simply complain and want to find solutions must ask ourselves: Why is it that Israel keeps losing the public diplomacy battle? What are we doing wrong? What strategy can help us win this battle? Israel's current strategies in public diplomacy can be summarized into two different schools of thought: the defensive school and the positive school.

The defensive school is an essential component of any public diplomacy strategy. According to it, Israel needs to dedicate resources to refute the claims made by the nation's enemies.

The focus of this school of thought is on contradicting Israel's critics. For example, if they claim that Israel is an apartheid country, people who adhere to this thought process will invest resources in explaining why it is not an apartheid country. Again, this defensive component must exist in any public diplomacy strategy, so the only question is how significant a part of the strategy it should be.

The main problem with giving this component too large a role in our public diplomacy strategy is that, while it is an important component, it is nowhere near sufficient. When acting defensively, Israel never sets the agenda. Israel's enemies set it, and Israel can only respond to it.

Also, the most powerful claim Israel can make using this strategy is to contradict the claim made by our enemies. For example, if Israel's enemies claim that it is an apartheid country, its most powerful claim according to this strategy is: "Israel is not an apartheid country." If Israel's enemies claim that it is an occupying force, its most powerful claim is: "Israel is not an occupying force."

If Israel were to use this strategy to its fullest extent, the most the state could gain is to convince its audience that it is not an apartheid country and not an occupying force. Saying that "we are not horrible people" is by no means an argument which is convincing enough to change someone's mind, or to convince anyone to start supporting Israel! Furthermore, in the likely event that we will not be completely successful in convincing people of our arguments, the spectrum of international public opinion will always lie between believing that Israel is an apartheid country and believing that Israel is "not horrible." This strategy might be essential, even vital. However, it is not enough, and by using only this strategy, we have lost the public diplomacy battle before it even started.

The second school of thought in Israel's public diplomacy tries to rebrand Israel by linking it to the state's many great achievements. A prime example of this strategy can be seen in the latest video produced by the Foreign Ministry.

The video, named "Created in Israel—Part of your life," tries to show the things which Israel has developed that have become a part of our daily lives. Thus, the video shows how Israel developed cherry tomatoes, flash drives and instant text messaging. It ends by reminding us that supermodel Bar Refaeli was also "created" in Israel.

Aside from the fact that I question the justification of spending public funds to get what amounted to around 100,000 views (many of which, if not most, came from Israeli news websites that reported on this video because it featured Bar Refaeli), a much more important question needs to be asked: Does this rebranding have an actual chance of succeeding? While speaking about Israel's achievements makes all of us who are already Zionists proud of these achievements, I doubt that it has the potential to convince the neutral observer.

The neutral observer hears all day long about the conflict in the Middle East, about the Israeli "occupation," about the claims of Israeli apartheid. When deciding whom he should support, Israel or the Arab world, the fact that Israel developed cherry tomatoes is not going to influence his decision.

Does anyone actually believe that the development of flash drives can convince someone to support a state that is supposedly a warmongering apartheid state? Of course not! Therefore, while these videos play very well within the pro-Israel community, their effects outside of these circles are minor and almost nonexistent.

Our whole strategy has to be different. Ask yourselves: Why do you support Israel? Many of you will feel the immediate instinct of connecting your support to your Jewish identity.

However, putting aside your Jewish identity, why are your feelings for Israel still positive? I imagine your answers will not be because Israel is not an apartheid country or because Israel created cherry tomatoes. Rather, your answer will be based on the historical rights of the Jewish people, on Zionism as the movement for the liberation of the Jewish people, or on other ethical arguments. These arguments rely on universal values such as historical justice, freedom and liberty.

These are the arguments that need to be made in order to win the battle of public diplomacy.

The rebranding that Israel needs is not as the creator of instant text messaging, but as a symbol of freedom in this world, as the consequence of historical justice being done.

We should claim: If you believe in freedom and liberty, you should support Israel. If you believe in historical justice, you should also support Israel! As mentioned previously, according to the first school of thought, the spectrum of international public opinion will always lie between Israel being an apartheid country and Israel not being an apartheid country. With this strategy, we are broadening this spectrum and including within it also people who will have positive sentiments about Israel.

Also, unlike the second school of thought, we are not limiting ourselves to technical achievement but are talking about ethical issues. Our enemies are always talking the language of values: military occupation, apartheid and war crimes. The only way to win this battle is by talking about ethics and values.

The only way to win the public diplomacy battle is to change our strategy, to stop focusing on defensive measure or on technical achievements, and to start talking about the great universal values that Israel represents. When people hear both sides of the ethical debate relating to the conflict, they will be able to see that values and ethics are on Israel's side. However, as long as we do not work to promote our ethical arguments, we will keep losing this battle, which is of increasing importance.

The Reasons for Israel's Failures in Public Diplomacy

The recent announcement of a European boycott of Israeli companies with activities in Judea and Samaria has once again highlighted the state of Israel's public diplomacy: failures keep on coming and the situation never seems to improve. Much to the contrary, the BDS movement keeps getting stronger, Europe intensifies its pressure on Israel, events such as the flotilla or the Goldstone Report portray Israeli soldiers as war criminals.

As someone who deeply cares about Israel, these constant failures push me to ask: what is Israel doing wrong and how can we fix our strategy to start doing things right?

Israel sells the two-state solution instead of selling Israel

Since the start of the Oslo peace process, Israel's diplomacy and public diplomacy has strongly shifted. Instead of promoting Israel and Zionism, all of our efforts have moved to advance the peace process.

While many supporters of the peace process might be happy with its advancement, this can in no way replace our claiming our rights to the land of Israel. In fact, as we stopped defending our rights and focused on the peace process, the Palestinians never stopped claiming their own rights. This caused a situation in which Palestinians were making strong arguments while Israelis were completely focused on something else, tipping the scale in their favor.

Even when the peace process failed, our arguments were still linked to it. We argued: Israel tried to get to the two-state solution, but the Palestinians are refusing. Our focus was on showing how the two-state solution is the right solution and that we are doing our best to implement it.

Regardless of one's political opinion with regards to the two-state solution, such a strategy is deeply flawed. By focusing on how much we care about the two-state solution, we are basically inviting more pressure from the world. After all, if we want to get out of Judea and Samaria so badly, then what are we doing there? If we have no rights there and we are simply trying to end the "occupation," then why are we even surprised when Europe decides to boycott us?

In order to start winning the public diplomacy battle, we have to stop making the "two state solution" argument and start talking once again about our rights to all of the land of Israel. Those who support the two-state solution surely agree that it must be the result of a process of negotiations with the Palestinians, and therefore, they, too, should refuse to relinquish our rights before even getting to the negotiating table.

Israel acts defensively instead of pro-actively

Much of Israel's current public diplomacy is focused on answering the accusations of others. Israel focuses on explaining why we are not an apartheid state, war criminals, or an occupying force.

However, by making these arguments, we are letting our enemies decide what the framing of the discussion is. Many times, the framing of the discussion is even more important than the discussion itself.

If the question is always "Is Israel an Apartheid state?", then we are losing the battle before even starting it! We need to pro-actively change the question and make it: "Is Israel a symbol of liberty?" "Is Israel a symbol of historical justice?" "Is Israel a symbol of Hope?" By taking control of the framing of the argument, by being proactive instead of defensive, we will be able to completely change the rules of the game, thus winning the public diplomacy battle.

We speak of technical achievements instead of values

The few times in which Israel is pro-active, it does so speaking only of technical achievements. Israel speaks about how its citizens developed cherry tomatoes, USB keys and ICQ. However, while these achievements are impressive and surely make us pro-Israelis proud, they are in no way enough to counter the arguments leveled against us, which are based on values.

Think about it: if you were presented with two sets of arguments on country X, one set claiming that it was an apartheid state guilty of war crimes, and the other set claiming it was a very innovative country, would you ignore the war crimes and support country X just because of its innovation? Of course not! You would say: your innovation is very impressive, but you have to stop being a war criminal.

This is exactly what the world is telling us: we do like your innovation, but stop the "occupation." Stop the "apartheid."

As long as we speak of technical achievements while the other side speaks of values, we have no chance of convincing the world to support us, and we will continue to see Israel's image deteriorate.

Rebranding Israel

The solution to Israel's public diplomacy problems is a complete rebranding of Israel, using all of the new technology out there to achieve it. We need to get public diplomacy out of its 2003 mid-intifada mindset and enter into the year 2016, when our enemies use much more sophisticated means to attack us.

This takes serious work; often this work does not show direct or immediate results, as it requires long-term strategies. It means stopping to preach to the choir and being proud when a Youtube video gets 100,000 views, with 99,900 of them being from people who are already pro-Israel, and thinking of real ways to rebrand Israel to the world. Unless we work to change Israel's branding from "occupation," "apartheid" and "war crimes," to relevant values such as "hope," "freedom" and "justice," we will never be able to win the public diplomacy battle.

As the results of Israel's public diplomacy failures become more significant, it is becoming more urgent for us to start changing strategies and to start winning this important battle.

Time To Fight Back
Against the BDS

Prime Minister Benjamin Netanyahu's 2014 speech at the American Israel Public Affairs Committee conference was historic.

For years, the centerpiece of any speech that Netanyahu gave on foreign policy was Iran. Sometimes, he would also mention the peace process. In that year, in his AIPAC conference speech, the centerpiece was the Boycott, Divestment and Sanctions movement and the new anti-Semitism it embodies.

Finally, after years of letting the BDS grow into the monster it has now become, the Israeli government seemed to be taking things seriously:

> Throughout history, people believed the most outrageously absurd things about the Jews, that we were using the blood of children to bake matzot, that we were spreading the plague throughout Europe, that we were plotting to take over the world. Yeah, but you can say how can educated people, how could educated people today believe the nonsense spewed by BDS about Israel? Well, that shouldn't surprise you either. Some of history's most influential thinkers

and writers—Voltaire, Dostoyevsky, T.S. Eliot, many, many others—spread the most preposterous lies about the Jewish people.

Today the singling out of the Jewish people has turned into the singling out of the Jewish state. So you see, attempts to boycott, divest and sanction Israel, the most threatened democracy on Earth, are simply the latest chapter in the long and dark history of anti-Semitism.

Equating the BDS movement with classical anti-Semitism is not only accurate. It is also a strategic shift for Netanyahu. Until then, he had reserved this strategic tool only for Iran, which he constantly accused of denying the Holocaust while planning another one. Then, the BDS movement received the same treatment.

Netanyahu went on with a clear mission from the leader of the Jewish state to all supporters of Israel: "Those who wear the BDS label should be treated exactly as we treat any anti-Semite or bigot. They should be exposed and condemned. The boycotters should be boycotted."

Enough with the passivity; supporters of Israel worldwide need to start fighting back against the BDS movement. Unfortunately, since this historic speech, it seems little has changed in the actual policy used in the fight against the BDS movement.

Our weapons in fighting the BDS

Israel has several weapons available when trying to actively fight against BDS.

First of all, there are the "softer" weapons. The ingenuity of the Israeli people and economic promise this brings to anyone who cooperates with them makes it hard to break ties with the Jewish state. In order to amplify the effect of this weapon, Israel needs to make it clear: Anyone who cooperates with the BDS movement will be blacklisted from cooperating with Israel.

No legitimacy can be given to the BDS movement. When the Europeans passed their "Guidelines," inspired by the BDS movement, the right response should have been to find an area in which Europeans want Israel's cooperation and to cut ties with them in that area. Israel cannot remain a punching bag in the scenario in which Europe gets what it wants out of Israel even as it cuts ties when it is not to their advantage. True diplomacy is not about making people happy, it is about making people work towards your interests even if it is by "tougher" means.

The "stronger" weapons available are the millions of supporters around the world who are ready to enlist in order to help Israel. Israeli supporters around the world are incredibly diverse. They are of different origins, of different ages, of different religions and of different political orientations. What is important, though, is that together they hold an incredibly powerful purchasing power. Some are well placed in the most influential roles of the international economy. Others are simple middle-class people who buy groceries at the supermarket. However, if together all of these supporters gave a very clear message and said, as Netanyahu asked of them, "We will boycott the boycotters," no corporation would dare rise against Israel.

A case study can be seen in a recent campaign by an organization I am involved with called Global Action for Israel. This organization, based mostly on Facebook, aims to unite and coordinate supporters worldwide in order to respond to attacks against Israel. If Israel is boycotted by a company, all members will boycott that company. If a country boycotts Israel, any corporation in that country will be a valid target.

On February 17, the largest bank in Germany, Deutsche Bank, was reported to have boycotted Bank Hapoalim for "immoral conduct" because of its involvement with building in Judea and Samaria. On that day, a campaign was started on Global Action for Israel.

Thousands of emails were sent to Deutsche Bank explaining clearly that if the decision was not reversed, all members of Global Action for Israel would contact their local banks and demand that they cut their ties with Deutsche Bank for cooperating with the anti-Semitic BDS movement.

After all, part of our power is that we are customers of our local banks. One day later, Deutsche Bank came out with a clear statement rejecting any boycott of Israel: "We wish to make it explicitly clear that Deutsche Bank is not boycotting any Israeli company."

The bank claimed that it had never intended to boycott Israel, but rather that a private customer requested that his investments not include Bank Hapoalim for the stated reasons.

Whether the explanation Deutsche Bank gave was accurate or not, the speed at which it worked to clarify its position and their now incredibly clear and their explicit stance against boycotting Israel show the power that Israel supporters worldwide have if they work together to counter any attack against Israel. Corporations, after all, think in terms of profits and losses. If they are convinced by the BDS movement that investing in Israel is a bad investment since their customers are boycotting Israel, it is dangerous.

However, if they are convinced by Israel's supporters that any boycott of Israel will result in great economic loss, no corporation would dare to boycott the Jewish state.

Realism and public diplomacy

There exist several outstanding public diplomacy organizations explaining why Israel is in the right. There is no doubt that this is necessary. These organizations need to keep doing the great work they are doing. After all, the basis of our own support of Israel is our conviction in the righteousness of this cause, not any cost-benefit analysis! However, at a time like now, when the BDS movement is using intimidation, disinformation and threats to get companies to boycott Israel, we cannot just think of the righteousness of our cause but need to add a layer of realistic economic incentives based on thinking how best to defeat those boycotts.

In the long term, the change in discourse and the paradigmatic shift that traditional public diplomacy organizations work towards is what Israel needs.

Let There be More Stephen Harpers

Former Canadian Prime Minister Stephen Harper was Israel's best friend among world leaders. His support was so strong that he seemed to be in a league of his own when it came to supporting the only democracy in the Middle East. However, his support should also be a cause for soul searching for the Foreign Affairs Ministry in Israel.

Israel's foreign policy cannot be seen as the forbearer of Harper's loyalty to Israel. His friendship towards the Jewish state existed despite its foreign policy.

Harper and the Foreign Affairs Ministry speak in opposing rhetoric. While Harper embraces the righteousness of the Zionist cause and the justice that Israel symbolizes, the ministry is busy using apologetic language.

If Israel wants more Stephen Harpers in this world, it needs to start studying what it is doing wrong and understand the framing through which Harper looks at the State of Israel. Only then will we be able to reproduce this framing amongst other world leaders. Only then will we get more Stephen Harpers rather than more boycotts and sanctions against Israel.

Ever since the start of the Oslo peace process, the Foreign Affairs Ministry has stopped defending Israel. Instead, it started defending the two-state solution.

During Oslo, with President Shimon Peres serving as Minister of Foreign Affairs and its architect, the traditional discourse of the ministry shifted dramatically.

Israel was not to justify its connection to all parts of the land, including Judea and Samaria, but rather it was to embrace the two-state solution and seek to implement it. Israel was not to attack its enemies diplomatically, but, rather, it was to highlight advances in the peace process.

This mind-set became so entrenched in the minds of Israeli diplomats that the ministry then became known as the "Foreign Affairs Ministry of the Two-State Solution."

Even after Israeli policy shifted away from the peace process, the diplomats kept pushing it forward. This not only caused bad relations between elected officials and those diplomats, but was also incredibly bad foreign policy.

As the peace process became completely irrelevant, instead of once again changing its framing and going back to defending Israel, the ministry pushed on with the very same framing. Instead of looking for other diplomatic possibilities, Israel kept arguing for the two-state solution, while blaming the Palestinians for the failure to implement it.

However, according to this policy, the solution was still the right one. It was still being pushed forward. The framing did not change.

The ministry became the place where people went to achieve peace, instead of a place where people went to help Israel.

The reasoning behind such a flawed strategy is clear. The ministry was so entrenched in that framing of the subject that it believed it was impossible to speak to the world in any other way. The only way to gain world support, the diplomats thought, is to embrace the two-state solution. The world, they thought, will support the side that best embraces the peace process and the two-state solution.

The real problem with this approach is that the very acceptance of the two-state solution means that Israel should not be in Judea and Samaria since in the two-state solution Israel needs to leave these areas. If Israel should not be there, it is thus acting as an occupying force. By using framing that accepts the two-state solution, Israeli diplomats invited international pressure and boycotts.

It is not surprising that during my time working in the Foreign Affairs Ministry, I heard many of Israel's own diplomats saying that the boycotts against Judea and Samaria might be good since they might pressure the Israeli government to "finally" reach a peace deal. Israel's own diplomats, when they needed to choose sides between Israel and the two-state solution, chose the side of the two-state solution.

This flawed framing of Israel's diplomacy will never create more Stephen Harpers.

It will just create more boycotts.

Harper's great friendship with Israel shows that this strategy was based on nothing more than pure conjecture.

When speaking about Israel, Harper never mentions the peace process. It's not that he opposes a solution — he supports the establishment of a Palestinian State. Yet a more pressing for him are ethical issues.

Harper sees Israel as an outpost of democracy in a sea of tyrannical regimes. As a supporter of democracy, he cannot reject the only stable democracy in the Middle East.

Harper looks at Israel as the front line in the war between Western free society and Eastern dark regimes. In this clash of civilizations, how can one not side with freedom? He speaks often of his total opposition to anti-Semitism. To him, singling out of the Jewish State is no different from singling out of Jews.

Anti-Zionism is the continuation of the horrible anti-Semitism that has plagued the world for centuries.

Finally, Harper also sees the story of the Jewish nation returning from exile after 2,000 years as a symbol of hope.

This romantic story between a nation and its land, which were separated for so long and are now reunited, is a source of great hope for many people, including Harper himself.

In short, the former Canadian prime minister embraces Zionism. He looks at Israel with the admiration that great Zionists do. The question of the Israel-Palestinian conflict is then viewed in the correct context and proportions.

To bring these thoughts to the practical sphere, a few principles can be outlined to guide the actions of Israeli diplomats in building positive support for the state:

First, Israeli diplomats should never differentiate between Judea and Samaria and the rest of Israel. The very differentiation between these areas assumes that our presence in Judea and Samaria is unjust and makes us look like wrongdoers. This invites both external pressure and boycotts.

Second, diplomats should learn to tell Israel's story without relation to the Israeli-Arab conflict. Israel's story is a story of great hope and can be inspiring to all people. Israel's strategic importance as an outpost for democracy and as the front line in the battle for freedom is something that is completely unrelated to the Israeli-Palestinian territorial conflict. We need to emphasize these things rather than letting ourselves be dragged to questions of borders.

Third, diplomats should use all the tools available to them to defend Israel's right to all parts of the Land of Israel.

This includes the Edmund Levy Report that justifies Israel's presence in Judea and Samaria. The reason is simple: Even if one believes in the two-state solution, shouldn't he want Israel to get to the negotiating table in the best possible starting position? In order to get to the best possible starting position, it is crucial to use all the tools we have in order to get there. Without doing this, we are once again inviting more boycotts.

Finally, diplomats need to stop playing defense and start playing offense.

Israel's goal should not be to justify itself against accusations of apartheid or occupation. Its goal should be to be the one to set the agenda. Once we set the agenda as a Zionist agenda, everything else will be seen from a different perspective.

This should be our goal.

If Israeli diplomats were to follow all of these principles, boycotts would be replaced by celebrations of Zionism, and international pressure would be replaced with international admiration.

Harper would stop being the exception to the rule, and instead, the standard for heads of state the world over.

Trudeau's Shocking Strategy

One of the most shocking responses to the terrorist attacks in Brussels in March 2016 was that of Canadian Prime Minister Justin Trudeau.

While the whole world was condemning the attack and pointing to it as an additional sign of the ongoing war between the Western world and ISIS, Trudeau came out and highlighted the fact that he does not consider his country to be at war with ISIS.

The free world is slowly uniting to fight the obvious evil that is ISIS. This is probably a fight where the division between good and evil has not been so clear since the war against Nazi Germany.

On the one hand, you have bloodthirsty terrorists who target civilians both in their own land and abroad. On the other hand, you have freedom-loving democracies.

Justin Trudeau decided to highlight the fact that Canada is not at war with the bloodthirsty terrorists. In this battle between good and evil, Canada has now decided to remain neutral. This is a clear departure from the moral stance embraced by its former prime minister, Stephen Harper.

One might think that Trudeau is acting strategically, seeing the rise in violence and trying to keep Canada from being attacked.

However, a quick look at the recent attacks shows that the pattern of violence is not necessarily directed toward countries that have been tough on radical Islam. Quite the opposite: Belgium has been notoriously open to immigration from Arab countries.

There is even a political party in Belgium called the Islam Party whose representatives have a stated goal of bringing Shari'a law to Belgium. Redouane Ahrouch, leader of the party, claims that the long-term goal of the party is to turn Belgium into an Islamic state. In the 2012 municipal elections in Brussels, they elected two representatives to the city council. Belgium did nothing to combat this trend.

Trudeau might theorize that being nice and open with bloodthirsty Islamists from ISIS might ensure the security of the Canadian people. However, recent experience shows that the terrorists interpret this only as weakness.

This is not a winning strategy.

The question remains: What is Europe to do in order to combat the trend of radical Islam in its own territory?

One thing it should do is to look at the Israeli experience and learn from it.

Israel is the only country that has, over the last decades, fought terrorists that come from its own territory. This experience has taught the Israeli people some valuable lessons, learned in the hardest of ways, which should be presented to the West.

As a response to the attacks in Brussels, Prime Minister Benjamin Netanyahu said,

> Terrorism does not develop from injustice.
>
> It develops from a murderous ideology, from the desire to destroy the enemy and to take over from him. I have already said many times that terrorism comes, not from occupation and not from frustration, but from hope—the hope of ISIS terrorists who want to create an Islamic caliphate in all of Europe.

This distinction is critical in order to understand how to fight terrorism. If terrorism comes from the hope of terrorists to defeat the West, then the greatest victory we can give the terrorists is to show them weakness.

This is why Israel has constantly demonstrated a resilience after every terrorist attack. When a terrorist killed someone in a supermarket in February, it took only a few hours for the supermarket to clean up and reopen. This might seem insensitive, but it is the secret to Israel's strength. We do not let terrorists dictate our way of life. We keep living and we do not let them enjoy their victories. If Europe wants to defeat terrorism, it needs to know that there will be more attacks in the short term, but that after every single attack, it needs to show great resilience and get things back to normal as quickly as possible.

Another lesson that Europe can learn from Israel is about the prevention of terrorist attacks. Europe has already started learning from Israel about its intelligence—gathering techniques. However, this is not enough.

During the second intifada, many people claimed that there was no way to prevent the constant suicide bombings that occurred in Israel. Ariel Sharon, then prime minister, disagreed and started an operation called Defensive Shield. The operation was a great success, with the number of suicide bombings going down drastically.

The operation was based on several clear principles:

First, Israel had previously withdrawn from some Palestinian cities where terrorists were left free to plan their attacks without being bothered. This reality had to change, so Sharon decided to re-enter the major Palestinian cities and to actively remove weapons from terrorist groups. This was a dangerous operation that put IDF soldiers in harm's way. In fact, 30 IDF soldiers were killed. However, Sharon understood that this was a necessary price to pay for the country's security.

In Europe, there are many areas where the police are afraid to even enter. The suburbs of Paris are known to be dangerous areas that tourists are told to stay away from. Next to Brussels, Sint-Jans-Molenbeek has been the base of numerous Islamic terrorists, who carried out both attacks in France and Belgium. At least three of the terrorists responsible for the November 2015 Paris attacks were from Molenbeek, and President François Hollande claims that this is where the attacks were planned. Several months later, Salah Abdeslam, a suspected accomplice in those attacks, was captured. The fact that Abdeslam was able to hide for several months in that area indicates that he also had accomplices who helped him.

When problematic areas like these exist, police must be proactive. The police force cannot leave an area because it is dangerous, but rather, policemen must be given the tools to enhance their presence in these areas. It might cause riots at first and create short-term problems. It might even put some of these brave police officers in danger. However, it is essential to the security of Europe.

The second principle of Operation Defensive Shield was to bring the fight to the terrorist's territory rather than wait to be attacked and play defensively. Sharon put a siege on Yasser Arafat's compound in Ramallah, which was cooperating with the terrorists. He brought the fight to Palestinian cities.

Here, in the case of ISIS and Europe, this means fighting ISIS not only on the European continent, and in cities where they have a large influence, but also in Syria and Iraq, where ISIS is in control. The fight there is critical to protect Europe. In the short term, the defeat of ISIS in Syria might actually motivate the group to carry out more attacks in Europe to compensate for their losses. However, in the long term, defeating them there will mean cutting their resources and ensuring they do not have the tools to carry out those attacks.

Prime Minister Trudeau of Canada might think he is doing the strategically sound thing by avoiding a violent fight between the West and ISIS. However, this is a losing strategy that shows weakness and encourages terrorist attacks.

Trudeau would do well to realize that the whole Western world is at war with ISIS, and that we need a winning strategy to beat this terrorist group both domestically and abroad.

The European Refugee Problem

Israel's opposition leader Isaac Herzog caused a ruckus when he suggested that Israel should lead the way in accepting refugees fleeing Syria.

The reaction was well justified. After all, Israel is a small country, and the dangers of accepting unlimited refugees is known to all.

However, the tone of those opposing the idea of granting asylum to refugees was as problematic as the idea to grant such asylum.

Those attentive enough could discern that the response of some Israelis was too similar to the response of various countries to the Jewish refugee crisis during the Holocaust.

"Zero refugees! Zero! Zero!" one could read in some comments to Herzog's proposal, in statements all too reminiscent of one made in early 1945 by a Canadian immigration agent who replied, when asked how many Jews would be allowed in Canada after the war, "None is too many."

In 1938, the Evian Conference was convened to try to find a solution for the increasing number of Jews fleeing Germany. Walter Mondale described the tragedy of this conference, which failed to find a proper solution, in these terms: "At stake at Evian were both human lives and the decency and self-respect of the civilized world. If each nation at Evian had agreed on that day to take in 17,000 Jews at once, every Jew in the Reich could have been saved. As one American observer wrote, 'It is heartbreaking to think of the . . . desperate human beings . . . waiting in suspense for what happens at Evian. But the question they underline is not simply humanitarian... it is a test of civilization.'" Of course, the differences between the Holocaust and the current refugee crisis are striking. In the Holocaust, there was a small minority population that was threatened with extermination. While there are such populations today in Syria and Iraq, such as the Yazidis and Christians, most refugees are simply people who were on the losing side of the war, some of them are even direct participants in the fighting and flee after they lose.

Yet, an instinctive response to automatically refuse any refugees whatsoever is misguided. Rather, a framework must be built by which Israel can properly evaluate whether to agree to accept refugees or not.

When thinking of such a framework, we must first ask: What are the dangers of accepting such refugees? There are, in fact, two such dangers.

The first is demographic. Israel is the one and only nation-state of the Jewish people. The world is a better place when Israel exists, and there is a strong ethical and moral argument for the existence of a Jewish state in Israel. If the refugees accepted to Israel would change, even slightly, the demographic balance in Israel, which is already quite delicate, it could endanger the very nature of the State of Israel. Israel should not agree to such a scenario, which would signify the disappearance of the only Jewish state and would be a historical and moral disaster.

The second danger is much more clear and present. Many of the refugees are sworn enemies of Israel. More than they hate those who caused them to flee their own homes, they hate Israel.

They hate the Jews. "Israel is the ultimate enemy," "Zionists are my enemy," "Israel is a colonial power"— these are statements made by Syrian refugees in Italy this week. Instead of focusing on their plight, they keep focusing on their hatred of Israel. Even if we were to assume that most refugees are friendly to Israel (a false assumption), those who aren't could become a serious security threat if allowed to enter Israel's borders.

These two dangers make it increasingly clear that Herzog's naive suggestion to simply accept all refugees was not only misguided but a further sign that Herzog is not fit to be the leader of the State of Israel.

Still, those who automatically reject calls for help without a more nuanced approach are also not fit for the State of Israel, with its unique history. At least in theory, if we could be 100 percent sure that the refugees accepted into Israel are not security threats but, rather, helpless refugees who would be grateful to Israel for accepting them, we should take in a limited number of them. This number should be as big as possible, but small enough so as not to affect Israel's demographics.

Should this number be 5, 500, 5,000 or 50,000? It is unclear. Demographers would have a say, and policy-makers would argue as to the exact number.

We are left with the security argument.

On this argument, we must defer to the policy-makers and security analysts, who have much more information than we do about every person requesting refugee status. One thing must be clear: the onus of proof must be on the refugee. If we are not absolutely certain before giving him security clearance, then we should not accept him into the borders of Israel.

Here, too, however, a clear initial "no" without further examination would be misguided.

Between Herzog's delusional suggestion and the popular outrage against it, one person was able to properly define the correct framework for deciding whether to accept refugees: Prime Minister Benjamin Netanyahu.

Netanyahu said in a press conference: "Israel is not indifferent to the human tragedy of the refugees from Syria and Africa. We have already devotedly cared for approximately 1,000 wounded people from the fighting in Syria and we have helped them to rehabilitate their lives," thus acknowledging the problem and expressing pride at Israel's participation in finding a solution.

"But Israel is a small country, a very small country, that lacks demographic and geographic depth," Netanyahu continued. "Therefore, we must control our borders, against both illegal migrants and terrorism."

Thus, he expressed the need to be extremely careful and to take into account the two main dangers when accepting refugees—demography and security.

This type of nuanced and balanced leadership is exactly what a country with a situation as complex as Israel needs.

JUDEA, SAMARIA, AND JERUSALEM

Giving Peace a Chance

Why is Israel, a country so well known for its innovative spirit, unable to think outside the box when it comes to the peace process?

Albert Einstein defined insanity as "doing the same thing over and over again and expecting different results." Since the dawn of the Israeli-Arab conflict, the world has adopted a single approach to peace: Find the right way to divide the Land of Israel among Arabs and Jews, and peace will come.

The British Mandate area was divided in the 1920s, establishing Jordan as an Arab state and Israel as a Jewish one. In the 1947 Partition Plan, the United Nations tried to further divide the land that was left in the Mandate. However, the Israeli-Arab conflict only intensified. Recent peace talks were more of the same. Each failure has led to yet another attempt at implementing the same two-state solution, while expecting different results.

Reviewing the history of the conflict necessarily leads to the realization that it is about more than a question of borders. The Jewish nation has a connection to the whole of the Land of Israel, while Palestinians lay claim to cities such as Jaffa and Haifa. Nothing Israel can suggest will suit the Palestinians, and nothing the Palestinians can suggest would be accepted by an Israeli prime minister. There is simply no geographical solution to this conflict.

In Israel, the political Left was traditionally equated with peace-loving principles, while the political Right was perceived as refusing any opportunity for peace. Additionally, the Right was often accused of not offering alternatives to the two-state solution.

With the continued failure of the two-state solution, the roles have reversed. The Right has fostered several innovative proposals, which, although flawed, demonstrate a willingness to think outside the box in hopes of peace. Still, the Left rejects all solutions other than the impossible: to implement a two-state solution.

Those attempting to discuss alternative solutions are heavily criticized and attempts are made to silence them. Shouldn't peace-loving be equated with those yearning to find and discuss a solution to end the conflict by any means? Israel is a country renowned for its innovation. Why not use this innovative spirit in its search for peace?

The great philosopher John Stuart Mill wrote in his famous work On Liberty that "we can never be sure that the opinion we are endeavoring to stifle is a false opinion." By silencing everyone who raises an alternative, we might be stifling the option that could bring us peace.

It is my goal in this chapter to help bring fair exposure to alternatives to the two-state solution, and a selection of these solutions is presented below. Like the two-state solution, these solutions are far from perfect. The ensuing discussion is my analysis of the pros and cons of each solution, including the two-state solution as one possibility.

I do not endorse any of these plans. However, I do endorse a fair discussion of all of them. This analysis is incomplete and some existing approaches are not included. However, my hope is that this short list of alternatives will allow for a fairer discussion of the diverse approaches to the conflict, help us embrace innovation rather than reject it, and reframe discussions of peace more broadly than the paradigm of the two-state solution.

If a fraction of the intellectual energy, political power and financial capital that has been invested in the two-state solution had been invested in exploring alternative solutions, we might already have achieved peace in Israel.

The Hotovely-Elitzur Plan (annexation)

Short description: This plan, supported by MK Tzipi Hotovely, President Reuven Rivlin (when he was an MK) and the late journalist Uri Elitzur, seeks to annex Judea and Samaria into Israeli territory.

In order to counter the demographic threat this poses, the first stage of the plan includes massive incentives for immigration of Jews to Israel, as well as the legislation of a constitution that will enshrine the Jewish character of the State of Israel.

Pros: This plan is based on the values of democracy, recognizing that the Palestinians should also have political rights and not being afraid to give them those political rights, even if they end up becoming a significant and powerful minority in Israel. Much of the opposition to this plan, even from the Left, appears to have racist undertones, as people seem to reject the idea of having a large Arab minority.

Cons: This plan is based on controversial demographic data and presupposes the success of several initial steps, including the successful immigration of over one million Jewish immigrants and the legislation of a constitution.

The Bennett Plan (conflict management)

Short description: This plan does not seek to end the conflict but rather to manage it better. Economy and Trade Minister Naftali Bennett argues that, on the one hand, we cannot annex the whole of Judea and Samaria for demographic reasons. On the other hand, the creation of a Palestinian state cannot be the solution, for historical and security reasons. His solution is to annex part of Judea and Samaria into Israeli control, while granting autonomy to the Palestinians in the other areas. This will include building new roads, which will enable Palestinians to live a completely autonomous life without feeling occupied.

Pros: This plan comes from a realist strategic perspective: the conflict cannot end; let us try to improve Israel's strength in this conflict. By not seeking a utopian end to this conflict, Bennett is able to ask what Israel should do for its own good.

Cons: This plan does not claim to bring about an end to the conflict. Palestinians will have autonomy, but not sovereignty. It is hard to imagine a scenario in which

Palestinians will agree to those terms and therefore, the conflict will continue to rage on.

The Israel Initiative (the Jordanian option)

Short description: Jordan was created out of the British Mandate for Palestine and more than two-thirds of its population is Palestinian. If so, the national ambitions of the Palestinian people can be reached through self-determination in Jordan, by giving all Palestinians Jordanian citizenship and negotiating a final peace treaty with Jordan.

Pros: There is strong historical justice to this plan since it will return to the original British Mandate framework and divide the land of the Mandate into two states, one Jewish and one Arab.

Cons: It is unlikely that the current Jordanian government would be willing to implement such a solution. Even if a Palestinian government were established in Jordan, it would have no incentive to allow for this plan to be implemented.

The Two-State Solution

Short description: This plan aims to divide the remaining land under Israeli control into two states, roughly based on the 1948 armistice lines.

Pros: This plan already has international support and if a compromise were to be reached, it would be fairly easy to implement.

Cons: This plan requires Israel to relinquish important parts of its historical homeland. It also requires Israel to take serious security risks by accepting very narrow borders. Additionally, it has been tried over and over again—and it has always failed. Every failure has brought bloodshed, and one can assume that further failures will bring further bloodshed.

Investing in the Alternatives

The main objection to any alternative to the two-state solution is that these are unrealistic solutions due to the lack of international support.

To respond to this claim, let me quote former Prime Minister Menachem Begin.

When asked, "How can you lead a policy of settlement expansion when the whole world is against such a policy?" Begin answered: "Has there ever been even a single Israeli representative who told any foreign official that Judea and Samaria (…) need to be an integral part of Israel? What criticism do you have against any foreign official when even Israel does not say that? Do they need to be more pro-Israel than what Israelis are?"

As long as we keep telling the world that the two-state solution is the right solution, they have no reason to doubt it! Therefore, as long as we ourselves refuse to look at other options, the only option on the table will be the two-state solution.

As we have said, this solution is not viable, and, therefore, as long as we refuse to open our minds and look at alternative and innovative options, peace will never be achieved. Those who truly want to give peace a chance need to start evaluating all alternatives, while trying to innovate and create further alternatives.

The Death of the
Two-State Solution

February 2016 will be remembered as the week in which the two-state solution died.

The month started with the Labor Party convention, during which the party officially endorsed a proposed change in policy suggested by its leader, MK Isaac Herzog. The proposal suggested that the party platform recognize the fact that the two-state solution is not feasible in the near future. While the Labor Party still believes in the two-state solution, it does not call for its immediate implementation anymore. When the leading left-wing party in Israeli politics no longer sees the two-state solution as an immediate goal, this marks its death.

The month continued with a funeral procession for the two-state solution. Several speakers from the Left and Right set out their views as to the correct course of action in the Arab-Israeli conflict.

Prime Minister Benjamin Netanyahu also spoke, and spoke directly to Herzog: "A year ago, I clarified that facing the great changes happening in our region and since all territory that is cleared is captured by extremists, it doesn't look like we can implement the two-state solution under the current circumstances. And then you attacked me."

Then, referring to Herzog's newfound pessimism regarding the proposed solution, Netanyahu said: "Good morning, Buji! I'm glad you woke up. Welcome to the Middle East."

If, on the Israeli side, there is a clear movement toward a prudent approach to the Israeli-Palestinian conflict which rejects quick fixes and utopian solutions and opens the door to a discussion of alternative solutions to the conflict, those who care about Israel should also seek to understand what is happening on the Palestinian side.

After all, conflicts have two sides, and unilateral solutions to conflicts are bound to fail. Therefore, a deeper understanding of the trends on the Palestinian side will allow Israelis to better assess what their next move should be, now that there is near-unanimous agreement that, at least in the short term, a Palestinian state will not be created.

The end of Mahmoud Abbas's rule

It is no secret that Mahmoud Abbas's rule over Judea and Samaria's Arab population is extremely weak. Many have claimed that if the Israeli army were not in the area to protect his leadership, Abbas would quickly lose power to Hamas terrorists or another competing faction. In such a delicate situation, and with Abbas turning 81 next month and nearing the end of his career, the most important question one must ask to understand the various scenarios for the future in the Palestinian Authority is: What will happen once Abbas no longer rules? In a recent interview with the Israeli press,

Jerusalem Affairs Minister Ze'ev Elkin, who serves on the security cabinet, set out four potential scenarios.

Either Abbas will have one successor from the Fatah movement, or there will be a Hamas takeover. It is also possible that a deal will be made between Hamas and Fatah for combined rule. Finally, in the scariest scenario, there will be no clear succession, and the confusion will lead to anarchy.

Anarchy in Judea and Samaria

Elkin believes that the last scenario is the most likely, and in such a scenario, since there would be no centralized address to communicate and coordinate with on the Palestinian side, the Israeli response to such anarchy would be very difficult to manage.

These various scenarios, and the likelihood of the disintegration of the Palestinian Authority, followed by complete anarchy, bring up critical questions for policy-makers: First of all, should Israel intervene in the internal affairs of the Palestinians in order to influence what will happen there in the next few years? If not, would the rise of complete anarchy warrant such an intervention? Add to that equation the instability of the Middle East as a whole and the rise of Islamic State, which is inspiring terrorist attacks even within Israel, and you have a recipe for real disaster.

How will Israel be able to control the free flow of weapons into Judea and Samaria from the Palestinian security forces to terrorist groups with no central address to be held accountable? Will Israel be able to properly defend Jewish communities both within Judea and Samaria and out?

Threats create opportunities

The threats posed by the instability within the PA and the unclear succession create a great opportunity for the Israeli Right.

For years, the Right has ignored the need to propose a clear alternative to the two-state solution, preferring to simply express opposition to the two-state solution.

Various solutions have been proposed, but no real and serious discussion occurred as to their merits. No real research was undertaken to foresee the economic, demographic and security implications of each. The alternatives were mostly suggested as a marketing technique to justify opposition to the two-state solution.

If only a tiny fraction of the money invested in furthering the failed two-state solution had been invested in studying alternatives, we would have a marketplace of ideas to discuss. We would not be left without any solution to implement in the short term.

The current situation, with a deep understanding on the Israeli side that the two-state solution is not currently viable, and complete instability on the Palestinian side, might finally give us a window of opportunity to look into and thoroughly study alternative solutions.

Unfortunately, as events are rapidly unfolding, there is very little time. Chaos in Judea and Samaria might begin soon, and Israel should know what its short—and long-term goals are before confronting it.

Only thus will Israel know how to react to Abbas's weakness, or to the eventual dismantlement of the PA. Only when we know where we want to go can we properly discuss the best way to get there. Only when we know the destination can we discuss the roadmap.

This is why Israel and its friends should immediately take a good look at all the possible alternatives to the two-state solution, now rendered obsolete. Once such a solution is defined, Israel will be able to better assess its relationship with the PA and the Palestinian Arabs.

Hope—More than a National Anthem

With each announcement of yet another round of negotiations based on the flawed two-state paradigm, I always express my opposition. After hearing my opposition, many of my colleagues look at me with puzzled expressions and ask: "Do you not have any hope for a better tomorrow?" I am a realist, and, as such, I think our foreign policy should not be guided by "hope," but by reality. However, characterizing those who oppose the creation of an enemy Palestinian state in the historical homeland of the Jewish people as not having "any hope for a better tomorrow" is misleading and superficial.

Hope for a secure Israel

Every time we have entered into a peace process with the Palestinians, the result has been increased violence. Oslo brought bus bombings; Camp David incited the second intifada. Even the unilateral disengagement from Gaza sent Kassam rockets to all of southern Israel. Why are we to believe that this round of negotiations will be any different? My hope is that Jewish mothers will stop burying their sons simply because enough pressure was put on the prime minister for him to make concessions that endanger Israeli lives. My hope is that it will be known that if the State of Israel is attacked, there will be significant repercussions against all those who threaten its security.

My hope is that this new level of deterrence will enable us to finally get some quiet here in Israel—an absence of war, or, in other words, the peace for which we have been longing.

Hope that the Jewish people will embrace their sovereignty

My hope, however, is not limited to the issue of peace. I hope that Israel will one day regain the courage to assert its sovereignty.

I hope that it will not be afraid to build throughout its historical homeland.

The return of the Jewish people to the land of Israel is one of the most inspiring stories ever told. After 2,000 years of yearning and exile, the Jewish people returned to their biblical homeland and the very cities of their forefathers: Hebron, Shechem, Beit El and, of course, Jerusalem.

These cities are now threatened by the creation of a Palestinian state and are referred to by proponents of this solution as "occupied," or, at best, "disputed."

My hope is that the dispute will end, and that after 2,000 years of exile we will finally gather the courage to act as a sovereign nation in our own homeland. I yearn for the day when our nation will be proud and courageous enough to defend the right of the Jewish people to pray on the Temple Mount, the holiest site in Judaism.

I yearn for the day when a Jew will no longer need the army's approval to legally purchase a home in Hebron.

It is a 2,000-year-old dream, and it is a much greater dream than the less than 100-year-old dream of the flawed two-state solution.

Hope for the Land of Israel and the People of Israel to finally realize their love

One of the most powerful metaphors in the Bible views the people of Israel and the land of Israel as a couple in love. This is one of the popular interpretations of *Shir Hashirim*, the "Song of Songs."

As the metaphor goes, the Land of Israel and the People of Israel fell in love, got married and realized their love when the Jewish people became a sovereign nation in the Land of Israel. However, this loving couple was violently separated by a third party, who tried to establish his sovereignty by stealing and raping the bride.

The separation of this loving couple seemed eternal. For 2,000 years, every single day, they dreamed of reuniting.

For 2,000 years, they prayed three times a day that they should meet again. For 2,000 years, every year, on the Ninth of Av, they mourned their separation.

Finally, after 2,000 years, they were reunited. They met once again, resumed their love and were incredibly happy.

This is the story of the Jewish people's love for the land of Israel.

Today, some suggest that we cut off part of this land, which we love so dearly, to appease those who want to kill us.

They make these demands without any guarantee that such concessions will solve any conflict.

Would a husband ever agree to amputate his wife's limbs to appease those who harass them? Or worse—would he agree to "share" his wife? Of course not! He would stand up and fight to defend her.

My hope is not for the establishment of a Palestinian state. My hope lies with the age-old dream of the Jewish people being eternally reunited with their land.

Hope—our national anthem

Interestingly, the founders of Israel chose *Hatikva*, or "The Hope," as the national anthem of Israel. While most people know the sections of the *Hatikva* that are today part of the anthem, most people do not know the full version of the poem.

In the full version, the poet refers to the Temple Mount, to the tombs of our forefathers in Hebron and to other historical and religious symbols that exist in Judea and Samaria.

Many academics claim that Zionism was inspired by the rise of nationalism in Europe. There is no doubt that they are right. However, without the age old hope of the return to Jerusalem, Hebron and Bethlehem, which fueled the Zionist movement, it would have never gathered major support within the Jewish nation.

This hope is what caused most Zionists to oppose the Uganda proposal, when some Zionists (including Herzl) suggested Israel be temporarily established in Uganda and not in the historical land of Israel.

This is the hope that inspired millions to return to Israel. This age-old hope is what encourages Israeli soldiers, to this day, to risk their lives to defend Jewish sovereignty in Israel.

Differences in utopias

The claim that those who oppose negotiations, which are based on a flawed and previously unsuccessful program, have no hope for a better tomorrow is simply baseless. We, like the proponents of the two-state solution, have utopias—we just have different utopias.

In the utopia of supporters of the two-state solution, Judea and Samaria are left devoid of Jews so that the Palestinians can establish their state. Then, according to their utopia, peace will come.

In my utopia, the Jewish nation will not run from Judea and Samaria but rather will once again embrace it. Jews will appreciate every day they get to live in their historical homeland and, because of their deep love for this land, will refuse to part with any of it. Peace with the Palestinians will also come.

However, it will come from local cooperation and not from the establishment of an enemy state.

You can decide for yourself which vision is more hopeful.

End the Occupation, Bring Sovereignty

A recent Channel 2 report showed the miserable life of some of the Palestinian workers who must go through the Kalandiya checkpoint every day, just north of Jerusalem, to enter Israel to work.

Some workers spoke about needing to wake up before 3 a.m. to begin work at 8 a.m.. The long wait at the security checkpoint makes it impossible to predict how much time they will wait, and they must therefore arrive there as early as possible.

When seeing this heartbreaking report about the hardships that the simple Palestinian worker goes through, many thoughts come to mind.

Of course, the first thought is one of the tragedy of the fact that we even need such a security checkpoint. If there were no terrorist attacks, Palestinian workers could go to work and back home in a few minutes, without needing to go through this daily horror. In fact, in the report, one could sense the frustration that the Palestinian workers had against those who led the latest wave of violence, which only made their situation worse. A second thought, however, is much more meaningful when trying to solve this problem. On the one hand, one must ask himself if Israel could not invest in making these checkpoints more comfortable for the workers who must cross them every day. On the other hand, if the utopian peace that the left so desires were to be achieved, and two states for two people were to be established, this would not simply be a checkpoint, but an actual border. Borders are much harder to cross than simple checkpoints, and the situation of these Palestinian workers would only worsen.

Judea and Samaria—occupied territories?

Since 1967, Judea and Samaria have been in limbo. The question arose of how to deal with these territories, which were not under Israeli control. Israel's official policy was to declare that these territories were not occupied, but rather liberated. They had been unjustly occupied by Jordan, in clear contravention of the San Remo declaration of April 1920, a century ago, and the British Mandate, which provided that all of the mandate's territory be used for the establishment of a Jewish state.

Still, Israel decided to apply the humanitarian aspects of the laws of occupation to these territories on a voluntary basis. This means that the tool that exists in international law called the "laws of occupation" is present and alive in Judea and Samaria, even if the land belongs to Israel.

The consequences of this status quo are unpleasant for both sides. According to the laws of occupation, it is almost impossible for Israel to expand its presence in these territories, unless it is done for security purposes.

The result is that Israel applies a discriminatory policy in which Jews are treated as second-class citizens in Judea and Samaria.

The Palestinians are also victims of this situation. All the long-term planning for these areas must be done according to the laws of occupation. The problem is that the occupation is by definition temporary and therefore the laws of occupation do not provide the necessary tools for proper planning. The legal system in place is one of the most defining factors in deciding whether an area can gain long-term economic growth and prosperity. How can a system thrive where, for example, buying land is an incredibly complex legal question? How can a system thrive under military rule, as in the case of Judea and Samaria? When Judea and Samaria are unable to grow and prosper, both Palestinians and Israelis suffer from the lack of growth.

Aside from these technical difficulties, there is also a more crucial question.

As long as Israel treats these territories as occupied, even if it declared that it is doing so on a voluntary basis, the main policy focus towards these territories will be one of separation. After all, occupied territories are not a part of a country's sovereign territory.

They also have a different legal system guiding them.

Going from separation to coexistence

The Left in Israel has long advanced the idea of peace through separation.

The way to achieve peace, according to the Left, is to separate Israel from a new Palestinian state that would be established in Judea and Samaria.

This way of thinking does not include Judea and Samaria as an integral part of the State of Israel, thus submitting it to the difficult laws of occupation.

It is this way of thinking that makes the Kalandiya checkpoint an true impenetrable border, further harming the standards of living of the Palestinians.

The Right, while in power for some time, has yet to propose a coherent worldview to compete with the two-state solution. However, the principles to which it adheres are clear: No to separation. Yes to coexistence.

Of course, Israel's top concern is security. In the example of the Kalandiya checkpoint, it is clear that a checkpoint is needed there for security purposes, and Israel cannot allow just any Palestinian to enter Jewish cities as long as terrorism remains a threat. However, since coexistence rather than separation is what we seek, then the Right should lead the fight for more decent infrastructure at the checkpoints that would make it more efficient and humane.

This is exactly what Uri Ariel, a hardline right-wing minister, said when he described the conditions at the checkpoints.

"Go and see how they stand and wait to enter Israel at the checkpoints. It's shameful and a disgrace to the State of Israel and to the security establishment.

People stand there in terrible conditions: in the summer heat, in the winter rains. Why can't we fix this?" he asked.

The answer is that we need a paradigm shift in policy making, one that moves away from the dream of separation from the Palestinians and starts working toward coexistence. "We are responsible for the region," Ariel said.

The legal changes that need to accompany this paradigm shift are very simple: Israel needs to end the occupation of Judea and Samaria and start implementing a policy of sovereignty. Many think that ending the occupation means pulling out of these areas. What it should mean, however, is taking full responsibility for what happens there by becoming the permanent sovereign power there, and stopping this unclear policy of claiming a right to the land on the one hand, while applying the laws of occupation on the other.

We liberated Judea and Samaria 49 years ago; it is time for Israel to move away from legal paradigms meant for temporary control of the land and to take full responsibility for what goes on there.

This will be good for Israel, and it will be good for the Palestinians,23 as well.

Standing Up for Our Rights

Imagine a country to which you had no personal ties but that others accused of being an apartheid state. This state was constantly condemned all over the world, and in the UN, for war crimes and human rights violations. Imagine if others claimed that this country was founded on colonialist principles and was accused of systematic racism.

In its defense, this state simply emphasized the fact that it is a leader in hi-tech and innovation, and that it invented things such as the cherry tomato, ICQ and the flash drive.

Whose side would you be on? This is Israel's image as seen in today's world.

When thinking about the Jewish state's public diplomacy, one must think about what the unengaged, ordinary non-Israeli sees, not what the educated activist sees. Today, Israel is violently attacked by its haters through vicious delegitimization campaigns; these are of course based on lies, but the ordinary, unengaged person does not necessarily know that. Israel's response to this campaign is simply unconvincing.

Israel needs to refocus its message and debunk the lies thrown at it, such as these accusations of war crimes, apartheid and racism. It must cultivate a parallel ethical discourse, one that is no less passionate than the one promoted by the supporters of the Palestinians, based on the principles of freedom, historical justice and legal justice. This discourse is the only way to compete with the lies thrown at Israel because, although they are lies, they are based on the deepest levels of human conscience and cannot be rejected without the existence of an alternative ethical foundation.

The moral case for Israel is a strong one; however, no one seems to be making it. As such, a moral person who doesn't actively educate himself on the conflict is fed a narrative which leads him to oppose Israel virulently.

A new wind blows in the Foreign Ministry

Deputy Foreign Minister Tzipi Hotovely surprised a lot of people in her first speech after taking office. The reason why people were surprised was not the right reason, though.

People raised eyebrows when Hotovely quoted parts of the Jewish scripture, and its commentators, when talking about Israel's right to the Land of Israel.

Yet the real surprise was a very pleasant change in Israel's core diplomatic discourse. For the first time in years, there was a high-ranking official in the Foreign Ministry saying: "We are just. This land is ours."

Hotovely said:

> Many times it seems that in our international relations, more than emphasizing the rightness of our cause, we are asked to use arguments that play well diplomatically.

> But at a time when the very existence of
> Israel is being called into question, it is
> important to be right. The international
> community deals with considerations of
> justice and morality. We need to return to
> the basic truth of our right to this land. This
> country is ours, all of it.

After years of going around in circles and trying to find diplomatic ways to get the world to love Israel without actually claiming what is rightfully ours, Hotovely asked that we start talking about these rights again.

The only way the world is going to accept Israel is if it believes Israel has a right to exist. As long as Israel is afraid to talk about its legal, historical and moral rights to its land, the world will continue to question its existence and will move closer to the Palestinians, who are not afraid to speak about their claim to the land.

Dan Margalit, a leading left-wing Israeli journalist who is very close to Hotovely on a personal level, said he often tells her: "You are right, we have rights to the land, but the Palestinians also do! Why not discuss this as well?" Hotovely answers: "I have never heard Palestinian Authority President Mahmoud Abbas talk about Israel's rights to the land. Why should I talk about theirs?"

Instead of trying to be neutral and shying away from controversial issues, Israel's diplomatic corps need to be pro-Israel. It might sound self-evident, but it is not. Israeli officials are not UN officials, they are here to advocate for the Jewish state, to defend its rights and protect its interests. In order to do so, they must stand up for Israel's rights, and only Israel's rights.

If they don't, Israel's rights will never be a part of the public discourse and we will be left with our current, warped situation, in which the Palestinians fill this vacuum by constantly attacking Israel and talking about their rights, while Israel is afraid to stand up for its own rights to its land.

The importance of the legal rights discourse

At the end of the day, the question of Israel's legitimacy comes down to the legal issue: Does Israel have a legal basis for its presence in Judea and Samaria? Israel can try to justify its stance with security concerns, but this will only bring the world to the conclusion that Israel had good reasons to temporarily break the law. The world will still see Israel as a state that is breaking the law, and in the long term it will not be able to accept this. After a few years, the world will say: "If you keep breaking the law, then despite whatever reason you might claim to have, you are still a criminal."

The truth is that Israel has an outstanding legal case to make about its right to the entire Land of Israel, including Judea and Samaria. After all, the last legally binding document relating to this area of the world is the British Mandate, which clearly states this area is meant for a Jewish state.

No other binding document was ever drafted: The Partition Plan was unbinding, and rejected by the Palestinians. The Armistice Line of 1949 was never recognized by the world. Judea and Samaria, in legal terms, lay there waiting for the British Mandate to be applied and for this area to be part of the Jewish state, the State of Israel. In purely legal terms, in 1967 Israel did not occupy a foreign land, but rather liberated Judea and Samaria from Jordanian occupation.

Those who claim there is an occupation in Judea and Samaria, including global bodies such as the International Red Cross, look at the world in a flawed way: If a shirt belonged to Johnny, and George took it by force, would it be called stealing when Johnny took it back from George? Would Johnny be called a criminal? So, too, Israel just took back what was originally meant to belong to it, according to the last binding legal document relating to this region.

A new hope

Hotovely started her term in the Foreign Ministry on the right foot, by making a precise diagnosis of the problem with Israel's diplomacy: Its tendency to prefer to duck the tough ethical questions rather than to stand up for Israel's rights and the values it represents.

Will her term in the Foreign Ministry be remembered as a time when Israel's foreign policy was revolutionized and returned to the right path? At the time of this book's publication, it is still too early to tell.

The Supreme Court's Gift to the BDS Movement

As the BDS movement has been making news worldwide, we must also look inside of Israel to see which groups at home also help further this global campaign.

A study published by Legal Grounds, a campaign advocating on behalf of the legal basis for Israel's legitimate control of Judea, Samaria and Jerusalem, points the finger at none other than the Supreme Court of Israel.

The argument set forth by Legal Grounds is convincing: While the government has had an official policy of rejecting the claim of occupation in Judea and Samaria since 1967, the Supreme Court considers these territories to be under occupation. This gives ammunition to those who want to censure Israel for illegal activities, by allowing them to cite Israel's own Supreme Court as a legal source claiming these lands are under occupation.

In the interest of full disclosure, I must point out that Legal Grounds is a campaign which I fully support and which I have helped in the past. Its agenda — attempting to change the discourse with respect to the legality of Judea and Samaria and to stand up for Israel's legal rights in these areas—is of great importance to me as both a lawyer and as an Israeli.

International law is unclear as to the legal status of Judea and Samaria, and Israel has good reasons to claim that these lands are not under occupation.

In fact, the Mandate for Palestine clearly defined these lands as intended for a future Jewish state. The Mandate recognized the "historical connection of the Jewish people with Palestine and to the grounds for reconstituting their national home in that country." This is the most recent and only binding legal document to address this area and stand to this day.

While many people claim that the 1947 Partition Plan was also a binding plan, this is completely false. According to the UN's own Charter (Articles 10 and 14), General Assembly resolutions are mere recommendations and therefore not binding. Even if we were to ignore that fact, it is clear that after the rejection of the Partition Plan by the Arab nations, Israel had no obligation to adhere to the plan.

After Israel's independence, Jordan and Egypt occupied parts of the British Mandate meant for the Jewish state— Judea, Samaria and Gaza. This was an illegal occupation since these lands were mandated to become part of a Jewish state. In 1967, Israel liberated these lands from foreign occupation. It did not occupy them.

This position was reaffirmed several times by Israel, including in recent history. For example, in the Annex to the decision "Legal Consequences of the Construction of a Wall in the Occupied Palestinian Territory" by the International Court of Justice (ICJ) of 2004, there is a summary of Israel's official position with regards to the status of Judea and Samaria.

Israel, it says, does not consider that the Fourth Geneva Convention "is applicable to the occupied Palestinian territory," citing "the lack of recognition of the territory as sovereign prior to its annexation by Jordan and Egypt" and inferring that it is "not a territory of a High Contracting Party as required by the Convention."

More recently, on July 9, 2012, the government-mandated Levy Report came out with similar conclusions: "Our basic conclusion is that from the point of view of international law, the classical laws of 'occupation' as set out in the relevant international conventions cannot be considered applicable to the unique and *sui generis* historic and legal circumstances of Israel's presence in Judea and Samaria spanning over decades.... Therefore, according to international law, Israelis have the legal right to settle in Judea and Samaria and the establishment of settlements cannot, in and of itself, be considered to be illegal."

In December of the same year, when a new government was formed, the cabinet passed resolution 5251:

> The Jewish people has a natural, historical and legal right to its homeland and to its eternal capital, Jerusalem....

> The State of Israel, as the state of the Jewish people, has a right and claim to areas, the status of which is under dispute, in the Land of Israel....

This has been Israel's legal position since 1967 and explains that Judea and Samaria cannot be occupied because they were not legally held by any sovereign nation beforehand.

This has been the official position of successive Israeli governments, both from the Left and the Right, while the Supreme Court developed a parallel doctrine.

The early years after the liberation of Judea, Samaria and Gaza saw the application of an interesting legal paradigm: The government rejected the *de jure* application of occupation law in Judea and Samaria but voluntarily took it upon itself to apply the humanitarian sections of the Fourth Geneva Convention.

Thus, Israel opposed the description of the situation as an occupation but found ways to properly handle the territories and to protect the rights of the Palestinians.

However, the court later ignored this important distinction. "Since 1967, Israel has been holding the areas of Judea and Samaria in belligerent occupation," the court said in one decision. "The Judea and Samaria areas are held by the State of Israel in belligerent occupation," in another.

In 2007, in the HCJ 9132/07 Albassioni vs Prime Minister decision, the Supreme Court held that the occupation of the Gaza Strip had ended, thus implying its agreement with the position that there existed an occupation in Gaza prior to the disengagement.

This was also expressed in A. vs State of Israel, in which the Court said: "A change occurred in September 2005, when Israeli military rule in the Gaza Strip ended and the territory ceased to be subject to belligerent occupation," differentiating Gaza from "the territories that are under the belligerent occupation of the State of Israel (Judea and Samaria)."

These sources are only a few of the many times when the Supreme Court falsely reaffirmed that the territories were under occupation, rather than specifying as it should have that Israel is voluntarily applying the humanitarian parts of Occupation Law in order to better the lives of the Palestinians.

The problem with the Supreme Court is not only that it is using an inaccurate doctrine. It is also not only the fact that in a democratic country, the Supreme Court should apply the legal framework decided by elected officials.

The real problem is the damage that these decisions do to Israel internationally.

For example, one of the greatest campaigns of the Boycott, Divestment and Sanctions movement against Israel is based on the security barrier, which it calls the separation wall. On this subject, the delegitimization movement against Israel achieved a tremendous victory when the ICJ decided the fence was in fact illegal.

Since then, those movements used this decision to justify their campaign and strengthen it. One must ask: What was the ICJ's case based on? The answer is simple: The law of occupation. And how did the ICJ reach the conclusion that there Judea and Samaria are occupied? After admitting that the State of Israel's official position was that there was no *de jure* occupation in Judea and Samaria, the court went on to claim that there were other possible interpretations. Then, to put a nail in Israel's interpretation's coffin, the court cited the Supreme Court of Israel calling it an occupation, citing the HCJ 201/09 Physicians for Human Rights vs Prime Minister ruling! In other words, the Supreme Court's clumsy characterization of Judea and Samaria became a tool in the hands of the delegitimization movement to attack Israel for allegedly occupying Judea and Samaria.

This is only one example of the many times BDS supporters and Israel delegitimizers cite the Supreme Court in their attacks. In many ways, the greatest tool that the BDS has against Israel is Israel's own Supreme Court, which fuels the BDS movement by contradicting Israel's official legal position.

The paper published by Legal Grounds sheds light on this fact, and policy-makers have to work hard to make sure that judges revert to applying the laws decided in Israel by policy-makers, as they do everywhere in the world, instead of offering their own interpretation of international law.

America's Quiet Boycott of Judea and Samaria

The European Union's call to label Israeli products from Judea and Samaria has received much media attention and widespread criticism.

The hypocrisy of the move is self-evident. After all, Europe labels products coming from the Western Sahara, a territory Europe considers to have been occupied by Morocco since 1975 with numerous Moroccan settlements, as "Made in Morocco." The labelling of products coming from parts of the Jewish State might therefore hide a much deeper contempt for the Jewish people, and is reminiscent of the times when Jews were themselves labelled with yellow stars on the European continent.

However, while the world's attention is turned to the European Union's worrisome declarations, many forget that policies of discrimination against Jews living in Judea and Samaria have been in place for far longer. I believe they have been in place for far too long.

The United States's boycott of Judea and Samaria

On this front, the actions of one country, purportedly Israel's greatest ally, are especially offensive. A closer look at the policy implemented by the United States

State Department shows a consistent pattern not of labeling products from Judea and Samaria, but rather of implementing a complete boycott of Israeli products from this region. This has been done under the radar, receiving very little media attention since 1967, with slightly more attention paid to this discriminatory policy since 1985.

Indeed, in 1985, the late Senator Jesse Helms of North Carolina questioned the Second Reagan Administration about its allocation of funds for Israel: "It is my understanding that when foreign assistance funds are disbursed to Israel, the U.S. Government requires Israel to sign a stipulation that none of the funds will be used for settlements on the West Bank. Is that correct?"

The State Department answered bluntly: "The stipulation requiring that foreign assistance funds provided to Israel only to be used in the geographic areas which were subject to the Government of Israel's administration prior to June 5,1967, has been the policy of every Administration since 1967."

It is important to note some further issues to fully understand how outrageous these statements are. America provides humanitarian assistance to many areas in the world, including the West Bank and Gaza (Judea, Samaria and Gaza). However, the assistance given to Judea and Samaria is given only to the Palestinian residents and not to the Jewish residents of Judea and Samaria. One example, the State Department's Middle East Partnership Initiative, rejected a grant proposal to provide support services to Jewish women living in Samaria whose loved ones were killed in terrorist attacks during the second Intifada. Those and other proposals are denied because the grantee was an Israeli community, institution or organization.

Also of note is the fact that groups trying to obtain funding for projects that encouraged the coexistence and cooperation between Jews and Arabs in Judea and Samaria were rejected. Some might argue that the reason for rejecting such projects is the fear that they would lead to normalization and turn what they wish to be an temporary "occupation" into Israel's permanent presence in Judea and Samaria. However, even then, one cannot deny that the bottom line is that the result of this policy is that, as soon as Jewish residents of Judea and Samaria are a part of these projects, it becomes impossible to get funding for that project.

In the past there have been a number of attempts to get the U.S. State Department to fund what are often called 'mom, flag and apple pie' coexistence and empowerment projects. For example, the Arab town of Salfit, roughly the same size as its Jewish neighbor, Ariel, had no water sewage treatment facility. With the help of a U.S. Agency for International Development grant, Ariel University could have developed the means to connect Salfit to the city of Ariel's sophisticated water sewage treatment facility. It would have been a win-win situation. However, the request was rejected. Whether the goal is to oppose the so-called "occupation" and its normalization, or whether the motivation for such actions lies elsewhere, the result is the same: an official American body's outright boycott of all Jews living in a certain geographical area.

In 2015, Barack Obama proudly signed a bill against the Boycott of Israel, as an amendment to the Trans-Pacific

Partnership. The amendment was to specifically mention "politically motivated actions to boycott, divest from, or sanction Israel" because of its policies in "Israeli controlled territories." However, the State Department refused this language, claiming that it "runs counter to longstanding US policy" toward Judea and Samaria. Spokesman John Kirby explained that US policy has consistently opposed settlements and therefore "does not pursue policies or activities that would legitimize them." In other—less politically correct—words, Kirby admitted that the US has no problem with the outright boycott of parts of Israel.

Standing up for our rights

The foundation for this boycott of Judea and Samaria is a misplaced belief that Israel's presence in these areas is illegal and that the areas are under occupation. While most of the international community has accepted the Palestinian narrative of the occupation of Judea and Samaria, Israel has continuously refused it, arguing for a different—and in my opinion more precise—reading of the law. This reading makes a case for Israel's right to the entire Land of Israel, including Judea and Samaria.

The last legally binding document relating to this area of the world is the British Mandate, which clearly states this area is meant for a Jewish state.

In international law, in order to understand to which entity a land belongs, we must look at the last legally significant event which occurred there.

The last legally binding document relating to this area of the world is the British Mandate, which clearly states this area is meant for a Jewish state.

No other binding document was ever drafted: The Partition Plan accepted in the United Nations was not binding and was rejected by the Palestinians.

The Armistice Line of 1949 was never recognized by the world. Judea and Samaria, in legal terms, lay there waiting for the British Mandate to be applied and for this area to become part of the Jewish state, the State of Israel. The Jordanians themselves insisted that language be included in the Rhodes Agreement that the armistice line should not be considered a future political border.

In purely legal terms, therefore, in 1967 Israel did not occupy a foreign land, but rather it liberated Judea and Samaria from Jordanian occupation.

Allies must stand together

As Israel is being attacked with threats of boycott worldwide, the time has come for the United States to right a historical wrong and to give a clear message to the BDS movement: "The more you try to hurt Israel, the stronger it will get."

It is specifically in a time when the BDS movement is pushing for a boycott of Israel that the United States' State Department should cancel its historic boycott of Judea and Samaria and embrace a more just policy of recognizing Israel's historical and legal rights to these areas.

Let My People Pray on the Temple Mount

One of the greatest infringements on civil rights in the Western democratic world has yet to gain the much deserved attention of human rights groups. It is time to let Jews pray on the Temple Mount.

Two years ago, in a lecture I attended at the Hebrew University's law school, a professor brought up the question of Women of the Wall praying at the Western Wall. The professor analyzed the famous decision by the Supreme Court lifting restrictions on women's prayers at the main Western Wall Plaza, as long as a proper alternative was provided in a similar location close to the Temple Mount.

The professor was incredibly critical: "How can we allow the fear of violence from a few ultra-Orthodox extremists dictate where one can pray or not? How can the fear of violence outweigh the most basic civil rights such as freedom of religion? This is outrageous! A democracy cannot function if it is being managed by fear of violence!"

With such a strong argument being made for freedom of religion, I thought someone in Israeli academia might finally understand the plight of the many Jews who are prevented from praying at the Jewish people's holiest of sites, the Temple Mount. I politely raised my hand and asked: "Your dedication to freedom of religion is inspiring. Would you not say the same thing about the current rules forbidding Jewish prayer at the Temple Mount?"

The professor was quick to disappoint me by dismissing my comparison. "No, the situation there is different," he said.

I asked: "How exactly is it different? On the one hand there is fear of violence. On the other hand there is the same basic right of freedom of religion. Where do you see a difference?"

I never received a response, as the professor ignored my follow-up question and continued with his lecture.

The current situation on the Temple Mount

Ever since the destruction of the Second Temple, the Jewish nation has striven to return to pray on the Temple Mount.

In 1948, after the establishment of the State of Israel, there was great joy at the return of Jewish sovereignty after 2,000 years of subservience to other nations. Yet this joy was incomplete, as most of Jerusalem, the eternal capital of the Jewish nation, was still under foreign rule.

Teddy Kollek, who became a secular mayor of Jerusalem in 1965, was asked to move the City Hall deeper into western Jerusalem. However, he refused, as he believed that the Jewish nation could never relinquish the dream of reuniting the city.

In 1967, the city was finally liberated. Motta Gur, the commander of the division that entered the Old City, famously said with a voice full of excitement: "The Temple Mount is in our hands! The Temple Mount is in our hands!"

However, ever since these few seconds of excitement, the Temple Mount has been far from resting in the Jewish nation's hands.

For all practical purposes, the Temple Mount is controlled by the Wakf Muslim religious trust, which forbids Jewish prayer at the site. At the same time, the Wakf actively destroys any archeological evidence of an historical Jewish presence on the mount to hurt the Jewish nation's claim to its holiest of sites.

Today, Jews are often barred from even entering the Temple Mount. Those who can enter are followed closely by guards who ensure they do not engage in prayers. If someone dares to pray, he is immediately arrested and barred from reentering the mount.

In most places in the world, such blatant discrimination would be condemned as anti-Semitic. However, in Israel it is justified. Jews are forbidden from praying in their holiest of sites, and people find this acceptable.

Where is Human Rights Watch?

One need not identify with the Temple Mount to accept that Jews have a basic right to freedom of religion. In fact, the infringement on human rights here is so clear that one wonders why human rights organizations are not lining up to condemn the Wakf for preventing Jewish prayers on the Temple Mount.

Imagine a small synagogue in Europe that was taken over by the government and where, with no wrongdoing by the Jewish community, the government forbade Jewish prayers. Can you imagine the outrage this would cause? How can one justify not applying the same standard to the Jewish people's holiest of sites?

The fact is that the only possible justification is fear. The world is afraid of the Muslim world's reaction to Jewish prayer on the Temple Mount, and therefore opposes it.

It is precisely the same dilemma civil rights activists have on many issues: Should their commitment to civil rights dictate their position, or should their fear of violence do so?

In general, human rights activists will reject the idea of letting fear of violence dictate policy. However, for some reason, when it comes to Jewish prayer on the Temple Mount, their position is different.

The current situation has now become one of the most serious breaches of civil rights in the Western world, yet it remains incredibly under-reported. When it is reported, those fighting for their civil rights are portrayed as religious fanatics with messianic fervor.

Those who care about civil and human rights should courageously unite around this important cause.

Between Independence Day and Jerusalem Day

At the time this chapter is being written, we are in the days between Independence Day and Jerusalem Day, when we celebrate Jerusalem's liberation in 1967.

On Independence Day in 1967, before the war started, Rabbi Zvi Yehuda Hakohen Kook gave what has now become a famous speech: "Where is our Hebron? Are we forgetting it? And where is our Shechem [Nablus]? Are we forgetting it? And where is our Jericho? Are we forgetting it?"

Those present describe Rabbi Kook speaking with great passion: "He spoke with a rage and fury that I had never heard before."

A few weeks later, these very same cities were liberated by the Israeli army, together with the Temple Mount.

It is now time for us to unite and scream: Where is our freedom to pray on the Temple Mount? Where are our basic civil rights as human beings? When will we, as Jews, be treated equally to other nations and allowed to pray at our holiest of sites? When will the State of Israel finally ensure that the Jewish nation is truly "a free nation on its land?"

Hopefully, our cries will be heard, for the sake of justice and for the sake of freedom.

Human rights organizations should join us in this important fight for freedom of religion.

Lessons From Gush Katif

Over 10 years have passed since the expulsion of Jews from Gush Katif settlements in Gaza.

Israel left Gaza unilaterally, hoping it would be a step forward toward peace. The opponents of the disengagement plan warned then that the plan was a dangerous adventure that would result in a serious security disintegration for Jewish residents of the South. They warned that rockets from Gaza would reach the cities of Ashdod and Ashkelon. Unfortunately, the last decade proved them right as Israel is still working to combat this threat.

Still, back then, in response, the supporters of the disengagement plan ridiculed these predictions. Meir Sheetrit, then a Likud Knesset member, said, "Some claim that there will be a threat to the cities of southern Israel. I have never heard such a ridiculous claim." Former MK Ran Cohen of Meretz said, "The disengagement is good for security." The late Ariel Sharon, who was then prime minister, outdid himself, pledging, "Ashkelon will not become the front line. Not Ashkelon, nor other places."

MK Orit Noked of the Labor Party claimed at the time that the disengagement would strengthen moderate elements in Palestinian society. However, only a few months after the disengagement, Hamas won the Palestinian elections.

The day before the beginning of the expulsion of Jews from Gush Katif, I was invited with a group of young Jewish leaders opposing the disengagement to meet with Israel's consul-general to Montreal. We knew our opposition would have little effect, but we wanted to express our thoughts to an official representative of the Israeli government.

We argued a lot and did not agree on much. However, in the end, I told him, "If there is one thing that we can both agree on, it is that we both hope that on security issues I will be proven wrong and you will be proven right. We both hope that Hamas will not be strengthened, and we both hope that Kassam rockets will not reach Ashkelon. I pray that time will prove me wrong."

Unfortunately, time proved that those who opposed the disengagement plan were right.

The unanswered questions

Some of the questions relating to the disengagement plan and Sharon's adoption of it remain unanswered.

How is it possible that the greatest supporter of the settlement industry became its greatest enemy? What caused Sharon to campaign against the disengagement plan proposed by Amram Mitzna, and to then implement a much worse plan? Furthermore, how were there no checks and balances in the country's political system to stop this complete flip-flop from occurring? The blows to democracy did not end there: While the opponents of the disengagement plan were exemplary in the methods they used to protest the plan democratically, the government's methods were of the very worst type.

How can one forget that in May 2004, Prime Minister Sharon promised to accept the results of an internal party referendum, and then completely ignored it after losing it? How can one forget that in June 2004, seeing he did not have a majority in his government, Sharon fired two opposing ministers in order to fix the vote and artificially build himself a majority? How can one forget the arbitrary arrests of minors based on unfounded claims that they were threatening the security of the country? How can one forget the way buses en route to legal protests were stopped, in what was a clear infringement of the right to protest and the right to freedom of expression?

These were the darkest years of Israel's democracy. This democracy, that we are so proud of for its ability to deal with the most complex situations involving the country's Arab population, failed the most basic tests when it came to its Jewish population.

On the day of the disengagement, I was working in an office in Montreal. My colleague, who was not Jewish, saw me constantly refreshing the front page of The Jerusalem Post website in great distress.

He asked, "What's wrong?"

I answered, "Things are happening in Israel."

He said, "Yes, I heard. But I don't understand something. Why would the Israeli government do such a thing to Jews? Is it not supposed to be the Jewish state?" Speechless, I looked at him in awe as I realized his innocent question was so precisely accurate.

"No, really," he continued. "Can you explain?"

Even today, 10 years later, I have no answer that can explain how the greatest democracy in the world failed to protect the rights of the very people for whom it was created.

Stop dreaming; examine the facts

The fact that so many people predicted exactly what the outcome of the disengagement plan would be proves that it was a foreseeable outcome. Yet, policymakers failed to face reality, then as now.

Why look at that dark reality in which terrorists will use every tool we give them to attack us, when we can live in an imaginary world where unilateral steps will lead to peace with enemies who have sworn to destroy us? The problem is that policymakers worldwide did not learn from the mistakes of utopians who refused to see reality.

In 2015, U.S. President Barack Obama signed a new agreement with Iran, which is based on nothing more than wishful thinking. The agreement allows Iran to keep its nuclear arsenal, rebuild its economy and continue to develop nuclear weapons, with no way for the West to stop it.

American leaders from both the Left and the Right were shocked by Obama's inability to properly assess the dangers of Iran's nuclear weapons program, and by the great risks he is willing to take with absolutely no guarantee in hand.

This bad deal is based on nothing more than a utopian view of the world, coupled with a deep desire for a strong presidential legacy following a term marked by gaffe after gaffe in international relations.

The problem is that utopian dreams rarely become reality. The danger of Iran's nuclear weapons program is very real, and Israel will need to decide how best to deal with this threat, which is a threat to the entire free world. Like many times before, Israel has been pushed to the front lines of the defense of the free world.

ISRAELI POLITICS

Why I support the Israeli Right

In every election cycle, the Israeli Left's strategy remains the same: Paint Prime Minister Benjamin Netanyahu and the Right as products of an inactive or reactive movement that never leads the way forward. "They've been in power for so long but have not accomplished a thing," they claim.

However, as much as the clearly left-leaning Israeli media try to push such an image of the Right, this image is at odds with reality.

The Right has been in power for the majority of the past two decades, this is true—but these decades have seen Israel grow in prosperity, thanks to smart governing by right-wing leaders. The times during which the Left has held power in these decades are the same eras that have seen security and economic problems. These issues have been left for right-wing conservatives to fix: the Oslo Accords, the evacuation of southern Lebanon and the disengagement.

Moreover, the Right is still trying to fix the various economic problems that plague Israel due to the socialist policies with which leftists have led the country since its inception.

While the Left tries to convince the world that "the Right does nothing, while the Left does," the truth of the matter is that the Left does bad, while the Right does good.

In the past, Netanyahu—along with Naftali Bennett, the right-wing economy minister—has pushed for important reforms that have advanced the Jewish state. As representatives of the right-wing parties in the current elections, the Likud's Netanyahu and Bayit Yehudi's Bennett have proven records of success.

This contrasts sharply with recent mishaps by the Left when its representatives have been placed in positions of power.

The Right improves the economy

The year was 2003, the middle of the second intifada. The economy was hurting, and Netanyahu was named Finance Minister.

Most finance ministers before Netanyahu had limited themselves to minor reforms. Setting himself apart, Netanyahu entered the post and immediately started leading the way towards dramatic changes—advocating for tax cuts, the privatization of many government-owned companies such as El Al, the national airlines, and Zim, the shipping company, as well as the reduction of various allowances granted to certain social sectors.

In this way, Netanyahu brought the economy from an incredibly unhealthy and unfair socialist vehicle to a much healthier free market.

Plenty of room remains for improvement, but the steps taken by Netanyahu were seen by all as revolutionary.

While today Moshe Kahlon takes full credit for the cellular revolution which increased competition in the cellphone service market, it was not too long ago that Kahlon himself admitted this revolution was pushed by Netanyahu. Thanks to Netanyahu's leadership, all of Israel can now save over NIS 200 shekels monthly on their cellphone bills.

In the field of transportation, every Israeli who travels on Route 1 from Tel Aviv to Jerusalem is witness to the massive renovations implemented under Netanyahu's leadership. In just a few years, Israelis will be able to go from Tel Aviv to Jerusalem by train in just over half an hour, a trip that today takes over an hour in traffic. The highway will also be extensively renovated, making it easier for those who still prefer traveling by car.

The unprecedented changes pushed by Netanyahu are, for the first time, making Israel a country where one can live in the periphery and work in the Center. While left-wing governments focused on subsidies to the periphery that simply act as temporary band-aids and do not solve any problems, the Right is bringing solutions.

Bennett continued in the tradition of Netanyahu.

When entering the Economy Ministry, he has led the way with serious reforms that have, in a very short time, already positively affected quality of life. In a groundbreaking decision, Bennett did what very few political actors are willing to do: he limited his own power to raise tariffs.

Though unexpected, the reasoning behind this unselfish decision is simple to understand and beneficial for all parties involved. Bennett understood that tariffs harm the local economy, and that he would not remain Economy Minister forever.

At the same time, Bennett lowered existing tariffs in some areas and worked to facilitate imports. The goal was clear: increase competition and lower retail prices.

As a result, in September 2014—for the first time in years—prices stopped rising and even began to drop.

These examples are only a few of the many accomplishments of the Right while leading the State of Israel. Even so, the Left keeps claiming that nothing is being done—complaining while the Right is busy getting things done.

Actually, in 2014, we had a small glimpse of the type of economic leadership the Left is proposing should it come to power.

Former finance minister Yair Lapid proposed a ridiculous plan to attempt to lower the price of housing. His "no value-added tax" housing plan was so absurd that not even one economist has come out to support it. Rather, his chief economist quit in protest, claiming the plan would cost Israel billions of dollars while raising demand for housing, thus increasing the prices of housing rather than lowering them.

This type of populist policy is what one would expect from the Left: policies that sound good in a Facebook status, but would never be backed by any reasonable professional.

The Left hurts Israel's security

If the Right is doing so much, how does the Left manage to convince so many people with its claim of right-wing inaction? The truth is that the underlying leftist claim when talking about the Right's inaction is not focused on economic issues, but rather on diplomatic issues. The Left is annoyed with the Right for not signing any peace agreement with the Palestinians, and for not evacuating the Jewish presence in Judea and Samaria.

After all, the Left did so much when it was in power! Leftists signed the Oslo Accords: giving the Arabs in Judea and Samaria full autonomy; bringing Yasser Arafat back to Ramallah; and enabling all the components necessary for the planning and execution of the second intifada—which resulted in over 1,000 Israeli deaths.

The Left also enabled Ariel Sharon's expulsion of Jews from Gaza, resulting in Hamas's takeover of the Strip, launching thousands of rockets into Israel, necessitating three military operations and culminating in dozens of Israeli deaths. On the northern front, the Left permitted the evacuation of southern Lebanon, which led to the strengthening of Hezbollah in the North, one serious war and the creation of one of Israel's most serious current threats.

The choice between the Left's actions vs the Right's justified reluctance for this type of initiative should be obvious. Israel cannot afford more "actions" of the type the Left is encouraging.

The choice is clear

The choice Israeli citizens have between the Left and the Right is clear.

They need to choose between an obsessive Left that wants to make further concessions to the Palestinians at all costs—even when unnecessary—and a Right that understands one must be cautious before compromising on security issues.

They need to choose between a Left that wants to bring back an economic system that hearkens back to the times of Socialism; and a Right that will keep moving the economy forward, freeing the market from government control and investing in infrastructure instead of subsidies.

The Right does good. The Left does bad. This is the reality.

For the good of Israel, let us hope that the Right continues to be the group tasked with implementing the state's actions.

Double Standards and the Hypocrisy of the Left

In the last few years, the Israeli Left has crossed all lines of reasonableness with its hypocrisy. This chapter will show some blatant examples.

Let us start with the "Israel as the Nation-State of the Jewish People" bill. The bill drew unprecedented criticism from the Left's supporters, both within and outside of Israel.

One of the central arguments made by the legislation's backers is that, in 1992 Israel passed "Basic Law: Human Dignity and Liberty," in which the Jewish state's liberal identity was entrenched. Since then, the courts have pushed Israel further away from its Jewish identity, falsely claiming it was contradictory to those entrenched liberal values.

Now, we also need to entrench Israel's Jewish identity in legislation, to bring back the delicate balance—which lies at the core of Israel as a Jewish and democratic state.

One of the Left's central arguments against the bill was that such central bills, which concern Israel's very nature, should only be passed with widespread approval. However, when examining the results of the vote on the previous Basic Law: Human Dignity and Liberty, one can quickly determine that agreement on that law was far from widespread.

Indeed, 32 MKs voted in favor of the law, and 21 voted against, in a Knesset made up of 120 MKs.

This means the majority abstained from voting.

Why is it acceptable for the Left to pass a divisive basic law, but the Right is not allowed to do the same?

The limits to legitimate art expression

Another example: A few years ago, in the middle of a wave of terrorist attacks, Amir Benayoun published a song on his Facebook page describing the story of an Israeli Arab who had Jewish friends and one day decided to kill them in a terrorist attack.

The inspiration for the song was a terrorist attack in which Arabs worked in Jewish businesses before attacking.

Benayoun was severely criticized for his song, as many claimed it had racist undertones that portrayed Arabs as backstabbing people. President Reuven Rivlin went so far as to revoke an invitation for Benayoun to sing at the President's Residence.

While I am no fan of the song, the ruckus it caused in the media is completely unjustified—especially when compared to the lack of media attention to far worse and more violent songs from the Left.

Why is it that songs inciting violence that come from the Left do not get the same scrutiny? Why is it fine for singer Mook E to call on people to "break the bones of the settlers?" Why is it not a problem for artist Yigal Tumarkin to say that, when he sees the ultra-Orthodox, he "understands the Nazis?" Is incitement only relevant when it comes from the Right? These two recent events are only some of the latest occurrences of a constant double standard, which is applied to the actions of the Israeli Right but not to those same actions by the Israeli Left. This systematic and hypocritical perspective is not only at the heart of the media's commentary on actions or policies pushed by the Right, but also influences the decisions of the courts and other decision-makers in Israel.

The court's relation to the settlements

As part of the effort to thwart the Gaza disengagement plan, settlers petitioned the High Court of Justice, claiming that the plan to expel Jews from their homes went against human rights.

In its decision, the court balanced two considerations: the right of people not to be expelled from their homes, and the right of the government to make decisions of diplomatic and security importance. The court's decision was that it was legitimate for the government to expel Jews from their homes for diplomatic or security reasons, and that the court would not interfere in such matters.

However, in another case with the exact same considerations, the court opted for the opposite decision. The question was whether the State of Israel could displace Arab populations in order to build the West Bank security barrier, which was intended to stop terrorism.

The state claimed that the route it chose for the barrier maximized its effectiveness, and that any change in that route would hurt national security. However, the court decided that the comfort of the Arab population was more important than the security considerations presented by the state.

Since these two cases dealt with the exact same considerations, the most logical explanation for the complete opposite decision in each case is that the courts hold a double standard in decisions they make relating to settlers, and in decisions they make relating to Arabs.

In fact, in another famous case, the courts rejected the claims of the state that wanted Route 443 to be closed to Palestinians (while giving Israeli Arabs access). The state claimed it would be too hard to ensure the security of Israelis on the route if it was open to Palestinians.

The court explained that it was the responsibility of the state to allow Palestinians access to this highway, and to protect Israelis. It was not reasonable, according to the court, to use security concerns as an excuse to make Palestinians take a longer way home.

However, when looking at locales under Palestinian control (Areas A and B), there are several roads that are completely blocked to Jews. Yet, the courts never forced the army to take the necessary security measures to allow Jews to take these roads.

In a 2014 conference about the role of the High Court of Justice in Israel, Dr. Ronen Shoval of the Im Tirtzu organization told a frightening story: In 2004, the state asked to destroy an illegal structure built by Arabs next to a road in Gush Katif, the Jewish settlements in Gaza that have since been destroyed. The courts refused to allow the destruction of the structure. Unfortunately, a few weeks later, Tali Hatuel, who was eight months pregnant, and her four daughters, aged two to 10, were killed on that road, shot by terrorists in that very building.

When contrasting this with the ease with which the court orders the destruction of illegal Jewish buildings in Judea and Samaria, Shoval tragically summed up the judicial decisions: "Yes to the destruction of the homes of Jewish settlers, no to the destruction of the homes of terrorists."

These are just a few examples of the double standard adopted by the courts when dealing with settlers rather than Arabs. It seems the courts in the Jewish state care much more for the rights of the Arabs than they do for the same exact rights claimed by Jewish settlers.

Double standards in public discourse

On October 22 2014, Meretz MK Michal Roisin wrote a Facebook post condemning Jews who had bought apartments from Arab owners in east Jerusalem. Even though these apartments were legally purchased, Roisin claimed that the very fact that Jews bought apartments in Arab neighborhoods made it similar to a nighttime burglary.

The problem is that, only 21 hours before, the same Roisin had written a post criticizing Safed Chief Rabbi Shmuel Eliyahu for calling on Jews not to rent houses to Arabs. Why are Jews not allowed to rent/buy in Arab areas, while Arabs should be allowed to do so in Jewish areas?

And yet another example: Ram Cohen, the principal of a school in Herzliya, defended a teacher in his school, Adam Varta, who criticized some of the actions taken by the IDF. Cohen defended the right of Varta to hold his own political opinions. However, this same Ram Cohen admitted he would refrain from hiring a teacher living in Judea and Samaria, because he does not agree with the Jewish presence in these areas. If it is permissible for Varta to hold left-wing political views, why would it not be legitimate for a teacher from Judea and Samaria to hold right-wing views?

Bringing honesty back to the political system

These examples outline the hypocrisy of Israel's political system, which holds the Right to different standards than it does to the Left.

Just as Israel is singled out and criticized by others for things other nations do, so, too, is the Israeli Right singled out and criticized for things the Left does all the time.

Things the Arabs are allowed to do are forbidden to the Jewish Right.

Fairness, integrity and honesty need to be brought back to the Israeli political system. The first step toward this is to stop the double standards against the Israeli Right, and to start treating people of different ideologies equally.

Nir Barkat as Prime Minister?

Nir Barkat, the popular mayor of Jerusalem, announced that he was joining the Likud Party, a move interpreted by many as a step toward an eventual run for the job of prime minister.

Many commentators responded immediately with opinions.

However, Barkat has yet to reveal any of his positions on the national agenda.

While many might find that he has been a good mayor, how can one support or oppose him without knowing what his plan for the country would be? What are the values that would guide him in making decisions? Israeli politics has been moving, in the past few decades, from a system based on competing ideologies, as defined by competing parties, to one based on a competition of brands, embodied by various personalities.

If there was once a clear difference between the socialist Labor Party and the liberal Likud, these differences have blurred with time. If the utopian peace process of Labor was once opposed to the realist security approach of the Likud, both parties now try to speak in each other's language.

Instead of having a battle of ideologies, we have various personalities battling one another without ever really describing their ideology. The question, then, in elections is not "what do you believe in?" but rather "who do you like better?" It is telling that, as Barkat now enters the Likud, no one is actually asking if his ideology is compatible with the party that is based on Ze'ev Jabotinsky's Revisionist philosophy, a well-defined, right-wing ideology.

This basic question is of critical importance in order to determine whether Barkat's move is the positive stepping-stone of an ambitious politician or a negative move by someone incompatible with the Likud, who is trying to use the Likud as a vessel for his own personal advancement.

The ideology of the Likud party

While it would be presumptuous to claim to be able to set out an ideology unifying all members of the Likud, or any other political party, it is clear that there are some guidelines that set out what the Likud stands for.

The party defines itself as "liberal and nationalist," two words that carry a very clear policy preference on various issues.

For example, on foreign policy, the Likud is a realist party. Jabotinsky's famous "Iron Wall" essay, written before the establishment of the State of Israel and calling for a strong hand to uproot the ambitions of Palestinian Arabs to kick the Jews out of the Land of Israel, is still a guiding document for senior echelons of the party. The Likud's charter officially rejects land concessions, and the Likud has traditionally opposed the two-state solution.

On economics, the Likud is free-market oriented. The Likud believes in a liberal economy, in the European sense, and was historically the antithesis of the Labor Party, which promoted a socialist economy.

Barkat has yet to reveal his agenda on national issues, and, therefore, when trying to define his ideology, we are left only with his record as mayor. This leaves us confused and makes it almost impossible to determine whether or not his ideology is compatible with the Likud's platform.

What does Barkat believe in when it comes to foreign policy?

On the one hand, Barkat is completely opposed to the division of Jerusalem. He has stood up against the destruction of Jewish homes in east Jerusalem, even standing up to the municipality's powerful legal adviser. However, he was also the campaign manager of the Kadima political party in Jerusalem. This was right after the disengagement, which he reportedly supported.

Does Barkat support the two-state solution?

Does he oppose it?

No one knows. Cynics would say that this inconsistent pattern means that he might look at the polls before making any decision on this issue.

What does Barkat believe in when it comes to economics?

On the one hand, he is a successful hi-tech entrepreneur, who has benefited from the free market.

One would expect him to believe in a competitive free market. However, as mayor, he ran things in a very centralized way. He defined projects and invested a lot of public funds in them, even if they were the type of projects usually left to the free market.

Was this done because he is a socialist who believes in an interventionist government, or was it done because of the truly complex nature of Jerusalem, which might warrant a more interventionist approach? It is unclear.

Should Likud members welcome Barkat?

The bottom line is that little is known about Barkat's policy preferences on national issues. Therefore, when people come out for or against him so early after his joining the party, they are supporting or opposing nothing more than an empty vessel, a brand, with very little substance in it.

It is unfortunate that people are already speaking of Barkat as a candidate for prime minister, when he has never filled any role on the national level. A more prudent approach would be to first ask him to serve as a member of Knesset, then as a minister, and only then to seek the highest office. After all, he himself has said many times that the secret to his success as mayor of Jerusalem was that he lost his first election, which forced him to sit in the opposition and learn the ins and outs of Jerusalem politics.

It should be noted that Barkat himself has never spoken of pretensions to the job of prime minister.

However, even if he does skip steps along the way, if Barkat wants to receive the support of Likud members, he needs to clearly outline his policy preferences and explain what his values are. Then, Likud members will be able to decide whether or not his worldview fits that of the Likud.

President Rivlin—The Great Deception

When President Rivlin took on the role President of Israel, he brought great hope to a large part of the population that was sick and tired of having the office used as a government enclave for promoting policies that a substantial part of the Israeli public doesn't agree with.

In fact, after years of losing every election in which he ran, Shimon Peres used his new position to promote his utopian view of peace through the two-state solution. The president became, not the president of Israel, but of this two-state solution.

Rivlin, a strongly right-wing individual with an impeccable liberal record and a deep respect for human rights, represented that on which most Israelis do agree.

The majority, as seen in election after election, believe both in human rights and in Jews' right to the Land of Israel. There is no contradiction. However, since being elected, Rivlin has changed his tone.

First, he started calling Israel a "sick society," claiming it was divided and suffering from racism, citing the actions of radical racist minorities. This was clearly a false depiction of Israel—after all, every society has problematic minorities that need to be dealt with, and singling out Israel is wrong.

Furthermore, this greatly hurt the Jewish state's reputation internationally and fueled the Boycott, Divestment and Sanctions movement by portraying Israel negatively and giving those who seek to delegitimize it ammunition from its own president! Rivlin also campaigned against the "Jewish nation-state" bill, claiming it was an affront to Israel's democratic character. Not only was this an unprecedented intervention in internal Israeli politics by someone who holds a purely symbolic role, but Rivlin's words were also published in English as an op-ed piece in *The Guardian*, encouraging international pressure against the bill. This international pressure once again fueled the delegitimization movement by encouraging an international campaign against Prime Minister Benjamin Netanyahu, who supported the bill, characterizing him as anti-democratic.

Recently, Rivlin spoke at the Herzliya Conference, again arguing that Israel is a divided society—pointing at two large groups, the Arabs and the ultra-Orthodox, as not being Zionist. This, according to Rivlin, is a danger to Israel's future.

The truth is more complex. While it is true that the Arabs and *haredim* make up a large part of Israeli society, and that they have traditionally chosen to live in their own respective communities, evidence shows that both communities are slowly integrating into the greater Israeli society.

Around 50% of ultra-Orthodox Jews in Israel describe themselves as Zionist; more than 50% of Israeli Arabs claim they want to do national service.

As such, Israel is not a society that is becoming more stratified, but rather one that is becoming less divided.

Once again, Rivlin's representation did a great disservice to Israel internationally, claiming large minorities are left out of the central public discourse.

The great hope of Israel's national camp becomes its biggest nightmare

If Peres was the president of the two-state solution, then Rivlin became the president of galvanizing the BDS movement.

Let's be clear: Rivlin is a great Zionist, a lover of the Land of Israel and a great opponent of BDS. In no way am I saying that he is willfully fueling this hateful movement.

How is it, then, that this is what happens time and again? The reason is simple: Rivlin's broad worldview, which includes a clear belief in Israel's rights to all of the Land of Israel as well as a strong willingness to integrate all parts of Israeli society, including Arabs, into Israeli life, is a great Zionist vision shared by many Israelis.

However, as president, Rivlin showed a great lack of courage in advancing his full Zionist vision, and instead focused only on the parts of it he knows the world will like.

Instead of courageously promoting his entire worldview, he selectively decided which parts to emphasize in order to stay internationally popular.

This leads to the warped vision that we now witness. Instead of speaking both of Israel's rights to Judea and Samaria and the need to integrate Arabs into society, Rivlin obsessively spoke only about the need to integrate Arabs and stopped there. In order to justify this obsession, he started developing a false doctrine about Israel being a "sick society," and opposed a bill defining Israel as the Jewish state. After all, there needs to be a reason for constantly speaking of racism, even if the great majority of Israelis are already strongly opposed to it.

His lack of courage made him one of the greatest tools of his own enemies, the BDS Movement, rather than pushing his true ideology.

A lesson for the Right

What happened with Rivlin should be a lesson for right-wing Israelis. On many issues, Israel's Right opposes the country's left-wing hegemony.

In academia, the courts or the media — the left wing still rules these strongholds, even when losing election after election. This was also true in regard to the presidency.

When faced with such a situation, the Right has two options: Either pass in-depth reforms changing the very structure of these institutions, to allow for competing ideas to be fairly represented, or try to overtake these institutions and rule them the way the Left has ruled them.

Essentially, the Right can either bring fairness to these institutions, or do to the Left what the Left did to it.

This question was relevant in regard to the presidency when Peres held the post—and used the office to push his political agenda.

Being completely symbolic, the presidency is not essential to Israeli life. The Right could have aimed to close down this useless institution; this also makes sense according to right-wing economic principles that oppose spending taxpayer shekels for no good reason. Instead, the Right tried to take the institution over.

The same question is critically important in relation to the courts. The Right has long complained of left-wing dominance in the High Court of Justice.

This is due to many systemic problems with the Israeli legal system; the process of nominating judges is unique, done behind closed doors, granting existing judges veto power over who the new judges will be. Israel's courts are also incredibly activist and intervene frequently in political decisions.

The Right can try to take over the judicial nominating committee and push for right-wing activist judges instead of those who are left-leaning.

However, as Rivlin has taught us, what the Right should do is fight for a systemic change: To change the way judges are nominated in Israel, and to stop judicial activism of all types—whether left or right wing.

Rivlin's example has illustrated that systemic problems should not be tackled by switching personnel who hold different ideologies, but rather by bringing systemic changes and deeper reforms.

THREATS
TO ISRAEL'S
REPRESENTATIVE
DEMOCRACY

Bring Democracy Back

Israel's democracy is threatened by internal elements that have stopped believing in the democratic process of majority rule and have started pushing forward their agenda by other means.

One of the few legislators in the Knesset who has constantly striven to protect Israel's democratic character is MK Yariv Levin of the Likud. At the time of the publication of this book, he is serving as Minister of Tourism.

The media response to his efforts has been atrocious: instead of thanking him for strengthening Israel's democratic values, he has been accused of threatening them.

A few weeks ago, during an annual conference organized by the Israel Bar Association, Levin announced that he would use his new role as coalition chairman to continue pursuing his legislative agenda of granting more power to elected officials, while limiting the power of courts to intervene in policy decision-making. Once again, Levin was accused of threatening Israel's democracy.

In order to allow for proper evaluation of the merits of Levin's proposal, I will provide an analysis of the various issues surrounding his agenda, including a brief discussion of the merits of democracy and some background on Israel's legal system.

Democracy's merits

Various forms of democracy have been around for more than 2,000 years. The term "democracy" itself comes from the Greek demokratia, which means "rule of the people."

In modern times, democracies have flourished as an alternative to various forms of non-democratic governments that existed around the world, from European monarchism to totalitarianism.

The goal of democratic reforms and revolutions is to take the power from an individual ruler and give it to the people.

In order for the people to rule themselves, they need a way to make decisions. Democracy, through majority rule, provides the framework for decision-making.

It is important to highlight the deeper meaning of democracy. While in other regimes, an individual or small group of people make decisions for others, in democracies the people rule themselves. In the age of nationalism, this idea translated into the ability of a nation to rule itself: self-determination.

In the case of Zionism and Jewish nationalism, democracy became the way that, after 2,000 years of exile in which Jews were ruled by foreign entities, the Jewish people could rule themselves and collectively make national decisions.

Judicial review in Israel

Modern Israel's early history was one of exemplary democracy. Every Israeli citizen had the right to engage in the democratic process, and every vote was worth the same, whether one was a regular citizen, a rich man or a judge.

In the early years of the State of Israel the courts would interfere in the democratic process only in order to guarantee its functioning.

For example, in the famous Kol Ha'am case, the courts intervened in a democratic decision to ensure that free speech, which is essential to the democratic process, would be guaranteed.

The right to judicial review exists in many countries around the world. This right gives the courts the power to cancel democratically passed legislation based on values expressed in that nation's constitution.

Since Israel has no written constitution, the courts have never had any right to judicial review.

There were attempts to legislate a constitution in the period of the state's founding, but they were unsuccessful. Rather, a decision was made to legislate "basic laws," which would be regular laws based on constitutional topics.

Once all the necessary basic laws are passed, the Knesset could then regroup these laws into a full constitution and pass it as such. Until then, nothing has made these laws any different than all other laws passed by the Knesset, aside from the title of "basic laws."

In 1992, the Knesset passed two new basic laws that dealt primarily with fundamental rights. In the landmark Mizrahi Bank vs Migdal Cooperative Village case, the High Court of Justice, led by Justice Aharon Barak, decided to interpret this new legislation as granting the courts the right of judicial review. Of course, nowhere in these laws were the courts granted such rights.

What, then, was the justification for the court's radical interpretation? Barak differentiated between what he called "formal democracy" and "substantive democracy."

Formal democracy is a type of democracy that he claimed to be completely technical, based only on the mathematics of majority rule, without any ethical claim. This, according to Barak, was not enough. True democracy also needs substantive democracy, where basic values and human rights are protected. Who is to protect these rights? Of course, Barak, being a judge, believed that only judges retain the mandate to do so.

In just a few sentences, Barak managed to completely reverse the meaning of democracy.

Majority rule became nothing more than a formal aspect of democracy. The deep ethical justifications for democracy's allowing for self-rule became obsolete.

Democracy became the rule of judges. Out went the great idea of the Jewish people gaining self-determination after 2,000 years of exile; in came the concept that "enlightened" people are the ones who need to make decisions on behalf of the nation. Democracy became nothing more than a new form of dictatorship led by judges. Prof. Ran Hirschl of the University of Toronto called it a "juristocracy."

Democracy and liberalism

The source of Barak's mistake comes from his inability to differentiate between two great ideas: democracy and liberalism.

While democracy is about self-determination through majority rule, liberalism protects individual rights and limits the government's ability to interfere in its citizen's lives. However, democracies can be non-liberal, and liberal countries can be undemocratic.

These are two sets of values, both of which are of great importance, but which are not identical.

For example, one can imagine a monarchy in which the king decides not to interfere unnecessarily in his people's lives. In fact, history has shown that some kings were quite liberal towards their subjects. On the other hand, a democracy can decide to elect extreme elements that will severely impact its citizens' human rights. One need only look at Egypt's new democracy to see a democratically elected government that is un-liberal.

The question then arises as to what is preferable: democracy or liberalism. As someone who believes both in democracy and liberalism, my answer is clear: democracy must always remain as the groundwork for decision-making. Liberalism must be advanced by democratic means. The Israeli Supreme Court decided otherwise, when it decided to hurt Israel's democratic character in favor of its interpretation of liberalism—an interpretation that is not even accepted among the various supporters of liberalism.

Protecting Israel's democracy

Recent academic studies by various professors such as Hirschl or Menahem Mautner of Tel Aviv University have shown that these recent attacks against Israel's representative democracy come from the elites who have become unhappy with the people's choices in elections. As long as democratic decisions brought about the government for which these elites yearned, democracy was legitimate in their eyes. Today, since the demographics of Israel have changed, the results of democratic processes are no longer acceptable; therefore, in their eyes, the final say must be given to judges who, because of their nomination process, have remained a part of these old elites.

The media, another bastion of these old elites, attacks anyone who tries to bring back the power to Israel's democratically elected parliament.

MK Levin, who is proposing to let Israel's citizens have the final say about what gets done in their country, instead of the judges, has been accused of attacking the state's democratic principles. Those who know about the real attacks that have been waged on Israel's democratic character by Israel's various elites know that what he is doing is quite the opposite: Levin is attempting to bring democracy back to the State of Israel.

Who really rules Israel?

One of the central questions that can help us understand whether a certain regime should be considered a democracy is: "Who is making the final decisions?" In a democracy, decisions are made by elected officials representing the people, thus allowing the people to rule themselves—even if it is done indirectly.

In a dictatorship, the people making the final decisions are not elected. In many dictatorships, you might still have elections, and even a functioning parliament. However, the final say on all issues is given to a supreme leader who is not elected. This leader can be a religious leader, such as the ayatollahs in the Islamic Republic of Iran. It can also be a secular leader, such as President Bashar Assad in Syria. However, this leader has the final veto power to decide what can or cannot be done.

It is important to note that, right from the start, what defines a regime as truly democratic is not the content of the decisions; dictators can make good decisions, while democracies can lead to horrible decisions. However, what defines whether a regime is democratic is the identity of the person making the decisions.

In Israel, intense judicialization of politics has made it almost impossible for legislators or the executive branch to make certain decisions.

This judicialization is characterized by increased intervention of the courts in political decisions. However, there is also another phenomenon which is no less important in this process, which takes power away from the elected officials and gives it to the bureaucratic branch of government. This phenomenon is the increased intervention of legal advisers in political decisions.

Let us look at the structure of the roles of legal advisers in Israel in order to understand how problematic it is and why it should be changed.

Veto power

Every government ministry in Israel has a legal adviser. This is also true in most other countries.

But the role of these legal advisers is defined very differently here in Israel.

There are various approaches to the roles of such advisers to governments around the world. In the US, for example, legal advisers act as the lawyers of the legislators for whom they work. Their job is thus to help these legislators implement their policies, by finding ways to defend them against legal attacks. These lawyers come and go with their bosses, as their role is deeply tied to their policies.

In most other countries, legal advisers to government are public service workers, who stay in government regardless of which government is in power. This is also the case in Israel. However, there is a big difference between what happens in other countries and what happens in Israel.

In other countries, legal advisers are there to advise officials as to what is legal and what is illegal.

Their advice is just what it sounds like: advice. The government can decide whether it wants to listen to this advice or not, knowing that if it doesn't heed the advice, it risks legal action in court. Of course, the government could have very good reasons to reject the advice of its lawyers, such as having received an alternative interpretation of the law which it feels is more accurate.

In Israel, legal advisers to government ministries have a formal veto power. This veto power was first established in a court decision and was then formalized in a directive by the attorney-general, which states: "The government is required to follow the directives of the legal adviser" (Directive 1.0000, February 16, 2003).

The effect of such a directive on democracy is clear. Decisions by the legal advisers are final. The government cannot decide anything which the adviser feels is illegal.

From legality to "reasonability" to "appropriateness"

If legal advisers in Israel would restrict themselves to commenting only on issues of law, then the problem we are describing would be minor. However, this is no longer the case.

In the last decades, administrative law in Israel has expanded quickly with the development of the idea that when the government does something which is "unreasonable," it is doing something illegal.

Of course, one central question comes up right away: Who is to decide what is and is not reasonable? If the government does something, it obviously believes it to be reasonable! Some people will say that the courts are better equipped to decide if something is reasonable or not. I disagree with them. However, at least when there is a court case, we hear about it. There is transparency, and the courts let us know why they believe something to be unreasonable in their decision.

Moreover, courts decide on policies after they have been implemented, and therefore have an incentive not to call them unreasonable unless they have good reason to do so.

In Israel, before being permitted to implement a certain policy, the ministry needs to get it approved by the legal adviser—who, as we said, has veto power. This means that if the adviser finds something to be unreasonable, he can make it illegal and stop the policy from implementation.

Let us ponder this for a moment: I happen to be right-wing and believe that it is completely unreasonable for a government in the Jewish state to kick out other Jews from their homes. If I am a legal adviser, am I really allowed to stop this policy from happening? Isn't that a breach of the democratic regime? On the other hand, my leftist friends believe that building homes in Judea and Samaria is unreasonable.

Some of them happen to be legal advisers.

Are they to be empowered to stop such a policy just because of their role? What is even more shocking and problematic is that the expansion of this veto power did not stop at "reasonableness." It has expanded even more.

Today, legal advisers feel free to use terms such as "unworthy," "unsuitable" or "not appropriate" when giving their opinion on issues. For example, Yehuda Weinstein, the former attorney-general and legal adviser to the government of Israel, wrote in an opinion on the candidacy of Rabbi Shmuel Eliyahu for Sephardi chief rabbi that the candidacy of this rabbi would be "unsuitable." Rabbi Yuval Cherlow, who is known to have had many debates and arguments with Eliyahu, came out against the legal adviser and said Weinstein had "crossed some serious red lines."

Not only do legal advisers have an unprecedented veto power that does not exist anywhere else in the world, this veto power is enhanced through the broad interpretation of administrative law in Israel via the concept of "reasonableness."

On top of that, legal advisers use their powers to go against things which they feel are "unsuitable"—even if they are technically legal! One starts to ask himself, what power is left with elected officials, and how can Israel still be considered a democracy?

Incentivizing "saying no"

The problem with the current situation is not only that it is undemocratic—it also hurts governability.

Studies in public policy have shown that one of the greatest obstacles to governability is the existence of veto players. This makes sense since as, when you have veto players, you can implement policies only when all are in agreement.

In Israel, with respect to legal advisers, the reality is even worse. Advisers are incentivized to say "no" to policy change.

The reason for this is simple. If legal advisers say "no" to a certain policy change, claiming it is illegal, their claims will never be put to the test. If they say "yes," they risk having their claims tested in court, since individuals might bring this policy decision to the High Court of Justice to argue against its legality. Therefore, the only way they will ever be proven wrong is if they say "yes" when they should have said "no." Saying "no" is always a safe bet.

This reality creates a situation in which it is impossible for ministers to govern their ministries. The public is then mad at its elected officials because it feels like government is not doing anything to improve their lives, when in reality government cannot do anything significant as it is always prevented from action by its own legal advisers.

Would the State of Israel have been established?

Zvi Hauser, Prime Minister Benjamin Netanyahu's former cabinet secretary, once argued in a lecture that, if David Ben-Gurion were to decide on the establishment of the State of Israel today, it is unclear whether legal advisers would allow him to do so. They would start asking: "Is it allowed according to international law?" "Is it a 'reasonable' thing to do?" "Why are you declaring in Tel Aviv? It might discriminate against another place!" and numerous other questions.

Ultimately, the advisers would decide not to make such a declaration, and Ben-Gurion would be forced to follow this "advice."

This extreme example illustrates the deep problems with the current situation. Not only are our elected officials unable to rule us and fulfill their purpose, but our government is also unable to function properly.

It is time for a change. It is time to bring back legal advisers to an advisory role—not a decision—making role.

Fixing Israel's Flawed System

One of the strongest arguments for supporting Israel in its war against radical Islam comes from the fact that Israel is the only democracy in the Middle East—surrounded by dictatorships.

While in Israel the ruler is a democratically elected leader representing the people, with a sovereign parliament, our enemies are led by tyrants.

Unfortunately, however, Israel's democracy has much to improve upon in order to properly function as a country in which the people rule themselves.

Much has already been written about the intensive intervention of courts and of bureaucrats in the decision—making process in Israel, who take power from the elected and give it to unelected elites.

However, the very electoral system currently employed is also extremely problematic. The system of proportional representation, supposedly the most democratic system, actually hurts the representation of the public.

The power of party membership

In a functioning and efficient democracy, parliamentarians view the general public as their employers.

They are the ones who define whether the parliamentarians will retain their job following the elections, and they are, therefore, the people whom parliamentarians try to please.

In Israel, things work differently.

Israel's electoral system is based on a proportional system. This means that each party presents a list of candidates for the parliament, and each party then gets a proportional number of seats, according to the number of votes it received in the general elections.

In such a system, what matters the most in defining whether someone will enter parliament or not is his placement on the party's list.

This means that the most important question for a parliamentarian who wishes to be reelected is who decides what position he will get on the list. The answer to this question defines whom he considers to be his employer.

In some political parties in Israel, one central person or one small committee decides where on the list each politician will be. This means that in these centralized parties, the "employer" of the parliamentarians are these specific people, and the parliamentarians will never do anything that would displease them.

In other parties, the "democratic" parties, party members at large decide who will be on the list through primaries. This is currently true of the Labor Party, the Likud and Bayit Yehudi. However, even if these parties are considered "democratic," and one might argue that their selection process is more fair than centralized parties, there are still significant problems with the primaries systems.

The reason is simple: most people in Israel are not party members. The largest party, the Likud, has around 100,000 members. This is far less than the nearly 1 million people that voted for the party.

Small party membership means that interest groups can organize within these parties and put tremendous pressure on the parliamentarians. After all, if they become members of the party, they become the "employers" of the parliamentarians.

In the last election, the difference between No. 18 on the Likud's list, which was considered a guaranteed spot in the Knesset, and No. 26 on the list, which was considered an improbable spot, was around 30 votes.

In other words, 30 organized votes can truly define the future of these parliamentarians. This gives a tremendous amount of power to these pressure groups.

In general, this should also make clear to all Israelis that, if they truly want to be a part of the political process, they should join political parties. However, most have yet to do so.

If party membership were wider, the influence of interest groups would more limited. However, as long as this system exists, the real "boss" of the MKs is not the general public, but rather the well-organized special interest groups within these democratic parties. This is not true democracy.

The division of power

This problem is compounded in a parliamentary system, in which the prime minister and all government ministers are themselves members of the parliament.

One of modern democracies' main principles is the separation of powers, which includes checks and balances ensuring that each branch of government performs in an efficient and just manner.

Parliament, according to democratic thought, is supposed to not only legislate, but also to oversee the work of the executive branch. In many parliamentary systems, where the executive branch also sits in the legislature, it is still possible for legislature to do this. After all, in a system like those of Canada or the UK, for example, where parliamentarians are elected in regional elections, they know that their "employers," the regional voters, want them to properly oversee the work of the executive branch, even if the prime minister is from their own party.

In Israel, however, the situation is different. As we said, the true "employers" of the MKs are those who decide what spot they will get on the party's list.

Let us ponder the effects of this on the separation of power. In a centralized party, like Israel Beytenu, this "employer" can be only one person, Avigdor Liberman. When Liberman was Foreign Minister, the people of his party were simple parliamentarians — did anyone really expect them to properly oversee and question the work done by the one person who can decide their political future? The outcome in democratic parties is only marginally better.

Even in democratic parties, party members are often very loyal to their party and despise internal criticism. Therefore, in the Likud, for example, if someone from within the party decides to criticize a Likud minister, they will probably be sanctioned in the next elections. Only in extreme cases, such as the release of terrorists or the removal of settlements, is such a criticism accepted and warranted. After all, party members want their party to stay in power, and they see such criticism as destructive.

This leaves the role of overseeing the actions of the executive branch solely on the opposition. The problem with that is twofold: First of all, the opposition has very little legitimacy since it is itself partisan. Secondly, the opposition in Israel is known to criticize all actions of the current government, without really analyzing the benefits of some actions, in order to paint itself as an alternative. This lack of nuance hurts its legitimacy even more.

As long as the link with the public at large is so weak, the important separation between the legislative and executive branches will be weak as well.

The solution

Solutions have been proposed to these problems.

Some suggest conducting the primaries in democratic parties on the day of the elections itself. The system would be simple—those voting for a certain party would also mention, with their vote, what their preferred list within that party would be. Of course, the party would have an internal system defining who can be a candidate on the list, but the order of the list would be decided on election day. This would make the MKs completely dependent on the general public voting on election day, and not only on party members.

While this idea would solve some of these problems, it would require a serious systemic reform. In my opinion, the real solution will come from incentivizing membership in political parties. The larger the parties are, the less power interest groups will have within these parties.

Incentivization can be accomplished by removing stumbling blocks to party membership and by having a centralized online system where people can easily sign up to join one party based on their ID number. Israel can also ask all voters to register for their party of choice when they register to vote, always giving them the option to register as independents. This required registration, I believe, would encourage most people to register for a party in order to enhance their political power.

Until policy changes are applied, it is the job of NGOs to ensure that the public knows the importance and the advantages of joining a democratic party that holds primaries.

Addressing Israel's Governability Issue

There is no doubt in anyone's mind that Israel suffers from serious problems of governability.

Ministers and Knesset members constantly complain about their inability to advance policy agendas. This creates a situation in which, not only are competent elected officials unable to serve their country properly, but in addition, incompetent elected officials have a great excuse for doing nothing. To compound the problem, this situation creates an atmosphere of lack of confidence in government, with many Israelis beginning to doubt the effectiveness of the democratic process.

However, frustration with the current situation should not rush us into an ill-planned solution. This has already happened in the past: exasperated by the lack of governability, electoral law was changed in 1992, mandating that Israelis would vote with two ballots — one for the Knesset, and one for the prime minister.

While the goal was to improve governability, this law ended up hurting it. Instead of strengthening the prime minister's role by giving him a direct mandate; the law created a situation in which people felt comfortable electing a prime minster without voting for his party in the parliament. This left the office of the prime minister without any parliamentary support. This legislative change failed, and the law was repealed in 2003.

The previous example demonstrates the problematic nature of any proposal to change the current electoral system. Small changes can have big, often unforeseen, effects.

Therefore, I want to go through what I believe should be the main principles that guide legislators when trying to fix Israel's governability issue.

Do not weaken the Knesset

The first principle is critical: Governability should not weaken the Knesset.

The Knesset consists of elected officials who represent the people of Israel. It is of course far more representative than the government since it includes the opposition.

A strong legislative branch is essential to a healthy system of checks and balances, protecting citizens from dishonest leaders. It ensures that leaders implement the policies for which they receive a mandate. If anything, in the current system, the Knesset is incredibly weak and unable to successfully oppose government bills. This is true because of the large number of small parties that would need to come together to build a successful opposition, and also because of the "party list" system in which Knesset members are required to show more loyalty to their party than to their electorate. In order to stay in the Knesset, they almost never oppose the policies of their party leaders, even when it is not the wish of their electorate.

The most obvious example of the Knesset's weakness versus an elected official's strength can be seen in the disengagement. In a healthy electoral system, a prime minister should not be able to be elected on an explicit promise to fight plans such as the disengagement, and then decide to advance such a plan. In a healthy system, Ariel Sharon should not have been able to implement the disengagement before first going to new elections. However, that is exactly what he did.

As a believer in right-wing principles, I do not want a new disengagement. I do not want a right-wing prime minister who changes his mind and starts supporting left-wing policies. However, the issues we are dealing with are systemic, and therefore both sides of the coin need to be looked at, and so I ask the leftist readers of this book: If a left-wing prime minister were elected, and one day, for some unknown reason, he decided to annex Judea and Samaria and build a number of new cities there, without going to new elections, how would you feel? In a healthy democratic system, a prime minister should not be able to do such a thing, and his main obstacle should be the checks and balances provided by the Knesset.

The improvement of governability should not come at the expense of the Knesset's power.

Strengthen elected officials

If this is the case, how should one improve Israel's governability? The truth is that the real cause for the lack of governability in Israel is much less popular than electoral reform. The cause lies in the relationship between elected officials and unelected bureaucrats.

In a healthy system, the elected officials decide, and civil servants implement. In Israel, the elected officials try to decide, but are obstructed by civil servants who see such initiatives as inimical to their own influence.

This is true in the case of legal advisers, who have a formalized veto power and can block any decision they believe to be illegal, even if they are wrong, without even going to court.

Legal advisers often have other motivations than purely legal ones for rejecting policy changes. However, it is also true of the Budget Department in the Finance Ministry, which can decide what money goes where, or of the Civil Service Commission, which decides who can hire personnel and when. It is also true of simple bureaucrats in various government offices, most notably perhaps in the Foreign Affairs Ministry, but also in ministries such as the Education Ministry, which knowingly pushes forward policy agendas that are completely at odds with the desires of elected officials.

Of course, they have the purest intentions and want to do the "right" thing. However, in a democracy, the "right" thing is for the people to rule themselves via their elected officials, and not for bureaucrats to make decisions and prevent policy implementation or policy change.

If someone wants to truly ameliorate the governability situation in Israel, his main focus should be on strengthening the position of elected officials and reducing the role of bureaucrats to policy-implementation rather than policy-creation.

Fight blackmail

That being said, one cannot ignore that our electoral system does have some problems and that the governability problems are not limited to issues of bureaucracy.

One of the major problems with the Israeli system is the presence of sectorial parties which do not have the national interest at heart but rather try to maximize what their sector gets from the government. This is often done through blackmail of the type: "Either you give me more than your opponent for my sector, or I will vote against you."

Truthfully, this is not foreign to government.

In America, although there is a two-party system, the same thing happens. The only difference is that it happens on a geographical level rather than on a sectorial level, with each house representative or senator trying to obtain more from government for the geographical area he represents. This leads to the famous pork barrel filled bills that America knows only too well.

However, the fact that this exists in other countries does not mean that it is not a problem.

Strengthen the link between the electorate and the elected officials

One of the most striking differences between the Israeli system and other systems comes from the lack of accountability in the Israeli system. In fact, many joke about the fact that there is no real word to translate accountability into in Hebrew.

This fact stems from a reality we hinted at before. The "party list" system by which electors choose between party lists and not actual people means that the elected officials are accountable to the people who decide who gets on the party list—not to regular citizens. These people can be party chairmen, party members or selection committees. However, even parties that let party members decide who goes on the list are not representative of the general electorate and are often overtaken by interest groups, be they political, ideological or economic interests.

Proper reform has to strengthen the link between the elected officials, individually, and the people who elect them in order to strengthen accountability. Many propose a regional system with counties, as in many other areas in the world. Other options are also available. However, one thing is clear: something must be done.

Cautious change

The issues of governability are definitely one area in which policy change would be appropriate.

It is my hope that future Knesset sessions will include an in-depth conversation about the consequences of the proposed bill, according to the principles outlined above, to ensure that the new system will enable citizens to vote for the government they want.

THE FREE MARKET, ECONOMICS AND SOCIETY

Zionism and Capitalism—The Quest for Freedom

A few years ago, in the closing lecture of a Hebrew University course on "Values in Israeli Society," the lecturer questioned the coherence of the values promoted by Prime Minister Benjamin Netanyahu and his Likud party. The lecturer explained that, on the one hand, Netanyahu was strongly attached to nationalistic values, which are collectivist values.

On the other hand, Netanyahu was also a capitalist, who believed in economic freedom, something associated with an individualistic outlook.

The professor who taught the lecture argued that this paradox could not be resolved, and therefore, Netanyahu was promoting policies that lacked coherence and direction. This was the closing message of his course. Unfortunately, there was, for some reason, no time left for questioning this thesis.

The fact is that nationalism and liberalism can coexist peacefully. History actually shows us that the places in which liberal economies flourished were places where there also was a strong sense of nationalism.

In this chapter, I want to argue that in the case of Jewish nationalism, capitalism is not only coherent with a strongly Zionist worldview, but rather that it is the most logical economic ideology to embrace.

Zionism is freedom

Jews have been yearning to return to the Land of Israel for almost 2,000 years. However, their yearning never led to actual political action.

What happened in the late 19th century for Zionism to turn into a successful established political movement?

With the start of the Age of Enlightenment, and, furthermore, with the development of liberalism, the idea of individual freedoms came to light. The argument was made that all individuals should be able to rule their own lives according to their own will and thus achieving personal freedom.

With the development of this liberal thought, the Jews also entered a period of "Jewish Enlightenment," known as the *Haskala*, in which they sought personal freedoms for themselves. As liberties were granted to all individuals across the West, the Jews, too, wanted to obtain those rights. Yet, very quickly, it became clear that in order to get those rights they would have to sacrifice their Jewishness. Various models were presented such as, "Be a Jew inside your home, and a man on the street."

However, they all failed, since Judaism is not simply a religion that can be confined to the home, but rather it touches all aspects of life—including national, historical and cultural identity. It is almost impossible to be fully Jewish while keeping Jewishness "inside," and many Jews were not willing to sacrifice their Jewishness.

Therefore, 19th century Jews, thirsty for the freedom of their Gentile counterparts, continued looking for other ways. Some considered complete assimilation. However, Zionism quickly became one of the leading alternatives.

If Jews could not get their freedom in Europe, maybe it was time to go back to their historical homeland and be freed there? Theodor Herzl, in his book *The Jewish State*, in which he outlines the initial vision of Zionism, put it plainly: "Perhaps our ambitious young men, to whom every road of advancement is now closed and for whom the Jewish state throws open a bright prospect of freedom, happiness and honor, perhaps they will see to it that this idea is spread."

The idea of freedom was the fuel that was meant to propel Zionism forward. Zionism was the movement for the freedom of the Jewish people, after failing to receive these freedoms in Europe.

Herzl's grandson, Stephen Theodor Norman, described the success of this movement beautifully after visiting what was then called Palestine: "You will be amazed at the Jewish youth in Palestine . . . they have the look of freedom."

Capitalism is freedom

Not surprisingly, modern capitalism was also the product of the European Enlightenment.

Adam Smith, the father of modern capitalism, was an important figure in what was called the Scottish Enlightenment.

Leaving aside the economic justifications for free markets, the moral justification is quite straightforward. Capitalists believe in smaller governments because they believe in freedom. Freedom stands in opposition to constraints and limitations. The bigger the government, the more constraints there are. More regulations equal more limitations. Therefore, a small government leads to more freedom for the individuals living in that state.

Most capitalists agree that some government intervention is necessary, as we are required to sacrifice some of our freedoms in order to live in a functioning society. For example, it is hard to find people who believe that the state should not run the national military. However, what differentiates capitalists from others is the value they place on freedom, as opposed to those other values which can be advanced through government intervention.

In fact, freedom is important enough to many capitalists that they are willing to refrain from intervening in citizens' lives, even if they are convinced that those people are doing the wrong thing. As Friedrich Hayek, Nobel laureate in the field of economics, said: "Our faith in freedom does not rest on the foreseeable results in particular circumstances. Freedom granted only when it is known beforehand that its effects will be beneficial is not freedom."

Milton Friedman, another Nobel laureate in economics and one of the most talented spokesmen for capitalism, also explained this clearly: "A major source of objection to a free economy is precisely that it . . . gives people what they want instead of what a particular group thinks they ought to want. Underlying most arguments against the free market is a lack of belief in freedom itself."

Capitalism, in other words, is a movement for individual freedoms.

People yearn for freedom

Academics often engage in impressive, in-depth analyses in which they classify different trends according to sophisticated concepts such as "individualism" and "collectivism." After studying these concepts so deeply and analyzing society within this framework, it is hard for them to release themselves of this way of thinking— and to see that other people do not look at the world through their eyes, but rather through common sense.

Therefore, when Israel's ruling party, the Likud, speaks both for nationalistic-Zionist values and for capitalist values, academics view it as a contradiction that is impossible to truly solve. They are unable to look at the values behind those concepts.

In fact, the truth is very simple.

People like freedom. People want freedom.

Israelis, including Likud members, also want freedom. They want freedom for their nation and they want freedom for themselves as individuals.

As such, they believe strongly in Jewish Nationalism and in Zionism, the national movement for the liberation of the Jewish people. And, as such, they also believe in the strength of capitalism and free markets to bring economic freedom to them as individuals.

This is no contradiction. Quite the opposite: If one of the core values of Zionism is freedom for Jews, then the most Zionist thing one can do is to encourage free-market economics in the Jewish state, so that its citizens will have maximum freedom! Yes, one of those movements is collectivist and brings freedom to the nation. The other is individualistic and brings freedom to the individual.

Yes, sometimes, on very specific issues, there is tension between the two sets of values.

However, the common denominator is stronger than what differentiates between them. This common denominator is, as expressed in our national anthem: "The hope of 2,000 years, to be a free people in our land, the land of Zion and Jerusalem."

The Land of Overpriced Honey

Every year, the Jewish New Year is welcomed with the famous tradition of eating apples and honey. Millions of Israelis go to supermarkets and buy honey in order to practice this custom which represents the wish for a sweet new year. Unfortunately, when Israelis get to the supermarket, the price tag on honey can often be reason enough to turn the holiday of Rosh Hashana (the Jewish New Year) from sweet to bitter.

Here are some facts: The honey market in Israel is about $150 million per year. However, two big companies, Yad Mordechai and Emek Hefer, hold around 80% of the retail market. In a market with such a lack of competition, it is no surprise that prices for honey in Israel are much higher than in other countries.

The average price for one kilogram of honey in the US is around NIS 40. In Israel, the average price for one kilogram is around NIS 54—an increase of about 35%.

Why is it that the price of honey in the Land of Milk and Honey is so high? How is it that the market is so centralized?

If the market in Israel were truly a free market, and with such artificially inflated prices, one would expect new players to come onto the scene—thus lowering the prices through competition. What, then, is stopping new players from entering Israel's honey market?

In this chapter, I will look at the various obstacles to true competition in the honey market. Many of these obstacles are representative of problems which exist in many areas of Israel's economy, and raise the cost of living and hurt the quality of life of the average Israeli. However, as we will see, the honey market is still an extreme case, with specific obstacles which do not exist in other markets.

Blocking local competition with regulation and permit requirements

The problems with competition in the honey market start with an odd rule requiring that anyone who wants to own hives for honey production must get a permit from an organization called the Honey Council.

To most people who are not familiar with honey production, this seems reasonable. Honey production is a dangerous business and dealing with hives seems to warrant a permit. However, a quick comparative look at the way the world relates to honey production shows that this rule exists only in Israel. In the US, France, Australia, Belgium and the UK, there is no such requirement. Rather, in most cases, the regulations require the hives to be a certain distance from public areas—without the need for a special permit.

Regulations are also aimed at stopping epidemics among bees, which have plagued many areas in the past. Honey production is also guided, like any other business, by tort law. Why, then, must Israel be different and require a special permit for owning honey-producing hives? This question becomes even more pressing when we look at the body granting these permits. The Honey Council is not a government body, but rather a private organization. The government gave this private body the right to decide who is and is not allowed to own hives and produce honey. This private council even decides who is allowed to enjoy the benefits of pollen grown on private farmlands. Farmers are not allowed to decide themselves what to do with the pollen on their own land.

As a private body, the Honey Council has its own interests and as such, has worked to limit competition in this sector of the Israeli market. For example, the council has the power to grant the right for bees to pollinate in certain areas.

However, in the past few years, the council made a conscious decision not to allow any new pollination areas. This makes competition in this market almost impossible.

This over-regulation, which is representative of many sectors of the Israeli economy, hurts the consumer— who is then the one who must pay for the market centralization. What is unique and especially appalling in the case of the honey market is that the regulation is enforced by a private body with private interests, rather than by the government, which supposedly watches out for the public interest.

Blocking international competition

One of the most obvious sources of competition for local producers of honey would be international competition. In an increasingly global world, there is no reason why international competition would not enable the lowering of product prices.

However, when it comes to honey, high tariffs make international competition completely irrelevant.

The price of the tariff on imported honey has been, since 2011, between NIS 12 and NIS 17 a kilogram. This is about the price of honey production in the international market, and is therefore close to a 100% tariff rate.

According to some bilateral trade agreements, there are some allowances for the import of honey with lower tariff rates.

Such agreements exist, for example, with the US and the EU. However, these agreements have a set quota of how much honey can be imported under that tariff rate, and it can only be imported by authorized resellers who then resell the raw honey as part of their own produce.

Therefore, even these trade agreements which are ostensibly intended to promote free trade do very little to enhance competition in the honey market in Israel.

In fact, the honey authority distributes the rights to imports under the quota—according to a company's size in the market. This method means that bigger companies get to import more, while smaller companies are only given the right to import quantities that are not economically viable. Thus, instead of leading to competition, the import quotas, compounded by the high import tariffs and regulations, end up causing further market centralization.

Time to reform the market

The problems with the honey market are not new.

In 1991, the state comptroller wrote in a report: "Since honey is not a basic need, there is no justification for a guiding hand [regulations] in this market."

In 1998, the state comptroller once again reported: "The Honey Council has a broad authority and leads to lack of competition in this sector. The lack of competition is the cause for much higher consumer prices compared to prices outside Israel."

Even the legal adviser to the Agriculture Ministry expressed opposition to the current situation: "Is there a justification for the violation of the right to freedom of occupation in the case of the Honey Council? This is doubtful.... Such benefits could be reached without the intervention of regulators, but rather through the free market."

For over 20 years, the problem with Israel's honey market has been known to all.

However, no one has yet fixed the problem.

The last few years of Israeli politics have been characterized by the Israelis' newfound consciousness of their country's economic policies. Israelis have had enough of paying more than they should for the products they purchase.

Unfortunately, some populist politicians tried to garner votes by calling on price regulation and price control. But the way to heal Israel's warped economy is to eliminate unnecessary regulation wherever it exists and letting the market determine price.

By allowing for a truly free market with free competition, consumers will be able to buy products at reasonable prices without hurting the country's economic growth. Actually, true competition will only lead to further economic growth.

Slash the Budget

Every time a budget is passed in Israel, after the dust settles from the negotiations, every minister starts discussing what he accomplished during those negotiations.

Let us look at the budget passed in August, 2015, as an example:

Miri Regev spoke of an unprecedented accomplishment for the Culture and Sport Ministry, with its budget raised by close to half a billion shekels, to over NIS 1b.

Naftali Bennett also took credit for increasing the Education Ministry's budget by NIS 4.9b.

Haim Katz took credit for raising the budget of the Ministry of Welfare and Social Services by NIS 1.3b.

Why is it that these politicians think they will encourage support from their electorate by announcing that they are spending more of our money on things we do not want? After all, if we wanted more cultural programming, we would buy more tickets to the theater or the opera. If the only way for them to get funding for these programs is to coerce the citizens of Israel to fund them through taxes, then there must not be much of a demand for them.

Most importantly, why is it that not even one minister came out and took pride in reducing the budget of his ministry? Why are we not hearing ministers talking about making their ministry more efficient—spending less money to accomplish more? Why are we not hearing ministers boasting of leaving money in the pockets of regular Israelis and letting them decide what to do with it, rather than letting the government decide? Israel has a strong economy, but it also has some serious problems within its economy.

However, the problem is definitely not that the budgets of the various ministries are too small. The problem, rather, comes from paternalistic regulation, which raises prices; state intervention in the free market, which also raises prices; and the lack of competition in many sectors, which, yes, also raises prices.

With the current model of thought, politicians just ask for more and more money rather than solving these real problems, and Israelis are left with less money and higher prices. By cutting spending and focusing on solving these real problems, Israelis would be left with more money in the bank and lower prices at the cash register.

Paternalistic regulation

Instead of concentrating on spending more of our money, policy-makers should work on removing paternalistic regulations that hurt the market and raise our prices.

For example, until recently, it was impossible to import soy milk into Israel. Why? Israeli regulators made it illegal to use the term "milk" for anything other than actual milk.

This meant that any international company producing soy milk would need to create a special line of products omitting the word "milk" in order to legally sell it in Israel. The result? A complete lack of competition in the market and very high prices for soy milk in Israel.

Naftali Bennett, as Economy Minister, abolished this ridiculous regulation. This is a step in the right direction, but much more is needed.

Recently, Israel's Health Ministry decided to rule against Heinz tomato ketchup, claiming that it is not ketchup! You heard it correctly: Heinz, which is almost synonymous with ketchup in America, can no longer call its product "ketchup" in Israel. The Health Ministry's s rationale is that not enough tomatoes are used in the ketchup to warrant the use of the word "ketchup," and that Heinz's ketchup should be called "tomato seasoning."

Of course, the body that pushed for this decision was Osem, Heinz's biggest competitor in the Israeli ketchup market. The decision is sure to bring the price of ketchup up, as the market now risks becoming a monopoly with little to no competition, where Osem is the only product on the market.

The common denominator in the examples of both soy milk and ketchup is a false belief that government knows how to make decisions better than private citizens. This is what pushes governments to decide for us, establishing ridiculous regulations that hinder our freedom to choose. Does the government not believe that we are smart enough to differentiate between soy milk and regular milk? Can we not read the ingredients in Heinz ketchup and realize that it is made of very few tomatoes? Instead of giving us information and letting us choose, the government is trying to decide for us. This creates serious problems in the market, raises retail prices and, of course, greatly hinders our freedom. These are the issues politicians should work to fix.

State intervention in the free market

A different example of intervention in the free market can be seen with price control.

Now, price control, in my opinion, is always negative. Price control warps the market and, while trying to reduce prices, actually ends up by substantially raising them. Much has been written on this subject, and yet many products' prices in Israel are still controlled, and politicians keep promoting the addition of other products to the price-control list.

However, one thing that is unique to Israel is a price-control law that tries to make sure the price of a product will never be too low! A few years ago, Israel passed the Book Law, banning discounts on new books. The claim was that writers were having a hard time making a living due to the low prices of books. Opponents of the law claimed that the law would hurt book sales; hurt new authors, who can count only on high sales to gain a reputation; and decrease the number of people who read books. This is exactly what happened.

At the book festival the year the law was passed, one publisher, Rotem Sella, challenged the law and offered a sale on new books he published. The result? Sella got fined millions of shekels.

Can you believe this? The government is fining a merchant for providing good prices to his customers! This, again, is an example of government trying to regulate something that should be left to market forces. If there are enough writers who want to get their art sold and read at low prices, then let it be. And if some authors claim to be on a much higher level that warrants higher prices, then let them try to sell their own books at those prices. The market competition will define what is true and what is not.

The good news is that MK Yoav Kisch of the Likud managed to reverse this draconian law, thanks to the support of the Minister of Culture, Miri Regev.

Stop taking money, start working

Ministers in Israel seem to misunderstand their job. When they arrive at a new ministry, they often believe that they are to represent the interests of those who are in this particular market. The Agriculture Minister will want to represent the interest of farmers, the Culture Minister will want to represent the interest of artists, and so on. However, ministers must represent the interest of all citizens of Israel with respect to a certain subject. This interest is not necessarily the growth of the particular ministry's budget. However, the exact opposite is often true.

Instead of taking more of our money, ministers should strive to make their ministries, as well as the market for which they are responsible, more efficient. This is a much more difficult job, since it means examining a lot of technical regulations, understanding the ins and out of economics and working against interest groups who benefit from market inefficiencies.

However, this is what the citizens of Israel should expect from their ministers.

Therefore, the next time a minister proudly speaks about growing the budget of his ministry, ask him why he is taking money away from hard-working citizens instead of working hard to justify both the money he is being paid and the mandate he received from his electorate.

The Government of
Israel vs. Aliyah

With numbers constantly rising, France has become, over the past few years, a pivotal country from which Jews immigrate to Israel. In June, 2015, five months after the terrorist attack on Jews at the Hyper Cacher supermarket in Paris, the heads of French Jewish organizations showed that 25% more French Jews moved to Israel in early 2015 than in the same period in 2014. In early 2014, already a record-breaking year for French *aliyah*, 4,000 French Jews emigrated; then, in early 2015, in the same months, 5,100 Jews made the move.

This migration is expected to grow in the wake of the latest terrorist attacks in France. While not specifically targeting Jews, these attacks have hurt French Jews' sense of safety, making the security issues of living in Israel less of a concern when deciding whether or not to move to Israel.

Recent polls have shown that a whopping 80% of French Jews considering moving.

France is the world's third-largest Jewish community, after Israel and the United States, with an estimated 500,000 Jews living in France today.

This means that 400,000 Jews are considering leaving France and moving to Israel. This is an unprecedented number.

Currently, the most generous estimates speak of around 200,000 French Jews living in Israel.

Bureaucratic troubles

Jewish immigration has always been a top policy priority for the State of Israel.

Indeed, this idea is entrenched in the Declaration of Independence: "The State of Israel will be open for Jewish immigration and for the Ingathering of the Exiles."

In recent years, there has been some vigorous discussions about whether Israel should continue to encourage Jewish immigration, or whether it should focus on strengthening its ties with local Jewish communities around the world. However, while there is disagreement about supporting aliyah, almost nobody argues with the fact that the gates of Israel should be open to any Jew who wishes to enter.

Why, then, is the State of Israel making it almost impossible for some French Jews to emigrate? Of course, on a formal and basic level, any French Jew who moves to Israel automatically gets citizenship. However, some of the hardships that certain expatriates need to undergo are completely unjustified.

For example, someone who has been a practicing dentist in France for several years has to go through a cumbersome process to practice in Israel.

In fact, some medical professions do not allow for any equivalent credit, and people who have studied for years in French colleges will have to start their education anew if they wish to make their career in Israel.

The reasons for these obstacles is that bureaucracies and regulations work in very strict and illogical ways. Unless the government has the goodwill to carve out the illogical exceptions from the regulations, they remain there.

Therefore, even as a huge wave of high-quality immigration is getting ready to come to Israel from France, the country continues to treat their diplomas as if awarded by third-world countries' education systems.

In some cases, the name used to refer to an institution ("college" instead of "university") can render the diploma illegitimate, even if in France such a difference is meaningless.

What is frustrating is that these issues have been known for years, and implementable solutions have been ready for a while, many prepared by the Kohelet Policy Forum. However, the legislative process on these issues, unless pushed by some motivated legislators, takes years, and the problems remain. Why do no powerful MKs or ministers, or even the Prime Minister, ask for an urgent legislative package to be pushed through the Knesset? If the draft bill and gas bill were pushed quickly through, why not this issue? Many countries would love to have these well-educated French Jews emigrate to their lands.

As long as the goodwill of the government is missing, the potential of a great aliyah from France might be wasted on procedural obstacles that make it too hard for French Jews to return home.

Contribution to Israeli society

Every new wave of aliyah, from whatever region, has had a profound cultural and economic impact on the state of Israel. It is this impact that has resulted in what we know today as Israeli culture. I believe that French aliyah has a serious contribution to make to Israel's culture, and that now is the time for this contribution to be made.

One of the toughest problems in Israeli society divides the country into groups: the Orthodox and the secular, the Sephardim and the Ashkenazim, the rich and the poor, and more.

Many joke, saying that if we did not have in the Arabs a common enemy attacking us and wishing for our destruction, Israel would be in the middle of several simultaneous civil wars. Of course, this is an exaggeration, but it is a telling one.

French Jewry has the exact same potential divisions, and yet, on a communal level, they have managed to make them disappear. Sephardim and Ashkenazim both remain culturally attached to their heritage in France. The religious and secular remain a part of the same community.

These divisions exist, but they are dealt with in a diverse community.

This communal level might not work on a macro-national level. However, people who grew up in this diverse environment can become leaders in Israeli society, making the strong divisions disappear.

This is the hidden potential of French aliyah—to unite the Jewish people in its land.

However, as long as government does not make it a true priority, this potential will be missed. It is our historic duty to make sure that the potential of French aliyah is completely fulfilled.

Synagogue and State

Israel's religious status quo is largely based on an agreement between former Prime Minister David Ben-Gurion and the country's Orthodox parties at the time of the establishment of the State of Israel.

Since then, Israeli society has greatly evolved: The ultra-Orthodox community has grown, the religious Zionist community has advanced to positions of great influence within the public sector, and traditional Mizrahi Jews have grown in numbers.

It is time to reject the status quo, and to start thinking about a framework that will define the relationship between religion and state.

Religion can influence policy

The first principle guiding the relationship between religion and state in Israel should be a complete rejection of the idea that religion should not have any influence on policy.

In a democracy, people vote according to their beliefs and conscience, and the source of one's beliefs should not matter. Why would it be legitimate for someone to oppose land concessions for historical reasons, but not for religious reasons? By insinuating that religion is not a valid source of moral beliefs to form policy, one is actually trying to silence religious people and remove them from the democratic game. Their opinions become irrelevant.

Civil servants should also be allowed to find motivation in their religious beliefs in order to be more effective at their jobs. Why should a secular person be allowed to be motivated by modern secular Zionism, while a religious person would not be allowed to be motivated by God? This issue has arisen several times in the past few years, when religious public servants mentioned God as a motivation for their service to the nation.

For example, during a recent war in Gaza, Col. Ofer Winter sent a letter to his soldiers before going into battle. He invoked the *Shema*, the traditional Jewish prayer of allegiance to the one God, and called upon "the God of Israel" to "make our path successful as we go and stand to fight for the sake of Your people of Israel against a foe which curses Your name."

For this, Winter was severely criticized by the left-wing media. But why should his motivation for defending his country be any less legitimate than a secular person's motivation? More recently, Yossi Cohen, the Mossad's new chief, was quoted as saying during a speech in his synagogue that Israel was created with God's help and needed God's help today. Again, this was widely condemned by the left-wing media. However, such statements are nothing more than expressions of the most basic beliefs of a religious person who sees Israel as a positive thing. Should religious people holding this belief be restricted from serving their country, even if they are the most qualified to do so? A person's religious beliefs should not be an obstacle to his serving his country. Moreover, it is undemocratic to claim that one's religious beliefs cannot influence his view of what a proper policy should be.

Politicians should not influence religion

While one's religious beliefs can and should influence his understanding of policy, it is unacceptable for politics to influence religion.

This is the basic foundation behind the American principle of the separation between church and state.

As Ben-Gurion himself put it: "The convenient solution of separation of church and state was adopted in America not for reasons which are anti-religious, but, on the contrary, because of deep attachment to religion and the desire to assure every citizen full religious freedom."

When the state provides religious services, it has to define what interpretation of religion it will accept.

This requires the state to enter the realm of religious interpretation in order to coerce people into accepting its interpretation.

Let us use the conversion crisis as an example: Israel's government currently controls all conversions made within its borders. This means that the government must decide what is a valid conversion and what is not.

Those who have a more stringent view of religion often criticize the rabbinate and oppose its conversions.

Those who have a more lenient view criticize the government for not being more lenient with conversions. At the end of the day, no one is happy and everyone is fighting. Instead of just allowing each group to follow its own traditions and beliefs, as was done for thousands of years without interference, the government steps in and decides which group is right.

The same is true of marriage laws, divorce laws, kashrut certification and more. Whenever the government interferes by deciding what is religiously acceptable and what is not, it coerces others to follow its opinion. This type of religious coercion is bad, not only for the secular who are not interested in religion, but also for the religious who are not interested in being coerced into accepting a certain interpretation of the law.

The current situation in Israel, in which the state controls many aspects of religious life, is very problematic and causes great dissatisfaction. Many studies have actually shown that countries in which government intervenes less in religious affairs have more religious people. This makes sense, since government intervention and coercion make religion less appealing and pushes people away.

The solution, therefore, would be to privatize religious services and free religion from control of the state. Remove coercion and bring more freedom.

This would also be good for religion itself. Right now, in order to decide what type of religious interpretation is accepted, the only relevant question is who has the most political power to compel others to accept his interpretation. If Shas does well in one election, it will decide. If Bayit Yehudi does well, then it will decide.

The question is about political power, not the content of the interpretation.

If religious services were to be privatized, there would once again be a free market of religious interpretation.

The question would not be about political power, but about the content of the interpretation: Who has the more accurate interpretation? Those with the most convincing case will be able to convince the most people. This would bring vitality back to our great tradition, which, thanks to this very same vitality, survived 2,000 years of exile.

One might try to argue that, in a Jewish state, religious coercion is necessary to maintain the state's Jewish character. Of them I ask: What is a more "Jewish" state? A state in which no citizens are allowed to use public transportation on Shabbat, causing many to use their own cars or hire cabs, or a state in which people are freed of religious coercion and many decide, of their own will, to keep Shabbat? A state in which marriage can only be performed by the rabbinate, and therefore many people go to Cyprus to get married, or a state in which the great majority of the population decides to get married in an Orthodox service of its own free will? Coercion takes all meaning away from religious observance.

Israel will be a more Jewish state when people choose to be more Jewish, not when they are coerced into being more Jewish.

The state should keep religious practice

That being said, it is important to differentiate between the actions of the individual and those of the state.

If an individual is free to do as he wishes, without coercion, the state should not be allowed to infringe on rights of religious practice.

This makes sense not only because Israel is a Jewish state and should keep a Jewish character, but also because state action always includes coercion, and by infringing upon religion, it discriminates against observant citizens.

It is of note that, in the previous example about public transportation on Shabbat, as long as the state subsidizes public transportation, taxes pay for buses to run on Shabbat.

This means that religious citizens are paying for what they understand to be forbidden by their religion. By allowing public transportation on Shabbat, the state is essentially coercing them into sponsoring the desecration of the Sabbath, which is unacceptable in a modern democracy.

Therefore, public offices should be closed on Shabbat. They should serve kosher food. Public transportation should not run on Shabbat, although one might devise a model in which unsubsidized public transportation would be allowed to run on Shabbat.

The state should be worried about religious coercion, but it should also be worried about secular coercion. As such, it should make sure that its own activities do not infringe upon religious rights.

Rethinking the status quo

Reforming the status quo is scary—no one knows what the result will be. Therefore, politicians on all sides have preferred to stick to the status quo since the creation of the state, avoiding important policy questions regarding the relationship between religion and state.

However, every so often, a story comes up that reminds us that the status quo is something that leaves everyone unhappy.

Israel has changed a lot since 1948, and it is time to rethink the relations between religion and state.

ISRAELI CULTURE

The Coalescence of
East and West

Israel's music industry is one of the most fascinating in the world, and an analysis of it can help us understand some of the phenomena that run deep within Israeli society.

One of the most successful Israeli singers today is Amir Benayoun. A few years ago, Benayoun, of Moroccan descent, released a record in which he took old Israeli songs and recorded covers for them. The result was powerful: The songs, originally recorded with a European touch, became infused with Middle Eastern sounds.

East and West merged into an authentic Israeli sound.

Benayoun is not the only Israeli artist who brings many influences together in his music. Idan Raichel is known internationally for his ability to bring together artists of various musical backgrounds to create a truly universal sound. To most international listeners, the result seems multicultural; to Israelis, there is nothing more Israeli than the music of Raichel.

Riff Cohen, for her part, recently defined her music as "Middle Eastern trash rock," incorporating influences from Western rock and the Levant.

This phenomenon is an expression of some of the deep sociological developments in Israel; a deeper study of it will help us gain an in-depth understanding of the Jewish state.

Arabic music in France

Ethnic music is not unique to Israel. Globalization has led to the intermingling of populations from different countries and backgrounds; audiences are exposed to music of different cultures. Many enjoy ethnic music and want to give it a place to develop in their own country.

However, in France, for example, a local may listen to Cheib Khaled singing Arabic music. But a French person will never say, "This is French music"—even if Khaled uses French lyrics and is influenced by French music. The Frenchman may like the sound of it, but he will always find it ethnic and foreign.

In Israel, when you hear Middle Eastern and European sounds merge together, it feels like truly Israeli music. No music is more Israeli than that of Benayoun or Raichel.

These days, when one hears music from other countries, it is because of globalization and the loss of identity.

If there was once a certain musical style for each country, in today's postmodern world, musical styles mix together as identity has lost its standing. Borders are not important anymore and thus musical styles from all around the world are found everywhere. Cheib Khaled may not be singing "French" music, but no one really cares about hearing "French" music anymore.

In Israel, the process is entirely different. As we speak, a particularistic national identity is being built.

Yet, there is a catch: This national identity includes influences from around the world. This is not because of the postmodern loss of identity, but because the identity of Israel is universal by nature; it incorporates aspects of identities from all over the world.

Postmodernism vs Hegelianism

Postmodern philosophy argues that there is no such thing as an objective truth and no way to know if a certain narrative is closer to or further from the truth— since there is no absolute truth.

Paul Karl Feyerabend (1924-94), an Austrian professor of philosophy at the University of California, Berkeley, gave an extreme description: "The only absolute truth is that there are no absolute truths."

The ideal postmodern political system is a multicultural society. In such a society, every culture has its place. No one culture is better than another; no one is closer to the truth. Every culture needs to be accepted as it is.

Hegelian philosophy is very different, arguing that different opinions can be valid, even when they are opposed. Hegel also argued that it is hard to contain absolute truth in one opinion.

But instead of saying there is no absolute truth, he focused on the difficulty in attaining an ultimate truth that does exist, saying it can be found in the synthesis of the different opinions: "Truth is found neither in the thesis nor the antithesis, but in an emergent synthesis which reconciles the two."

Israel's melting pot

As the in-gathering of the exiles began and the Jewish nation returned to Israel, there was serious disagreement between the Zionist movement leaders as to what to do with the strong cultural differences between the immigrants. Some wanted a "melting pot" to allow for creation of a new *Sabra*. Others wanted each cultural group to keep its own identity.

Ze'ev Jabotinsky was one of the great opponents of the melting pot:

> Those who know that I favor rapprochement between Sephardim and Ashkenazim will perhaps be surprised when I tell them that I am against forced internal assimilation, which aims to create a common Israeli identity, even if it is in the more distant future.
>
> There are different shades in all great nations, each of its parts has its own special advantages, and these I believe need to be preserved and developed—and not buried in a melting pot.

David Ben-Gurion, on the other hand, was a great supporter of creating a melting pot society:

> In the melting pot of Jewish brotherhood and military discipline, a new foreign

immigrant can be added in one night. He
can be refined and purified of his foreign
identity. This means the ethnic divisions will
be erased and the national brotherhood will
be revived as in the nation's youth, drawing
from ancient sources.

Since Ben-Gurion became prime minister, his opinion
became official Israeli policy.

But both those thinkers have ignored a third option,
which, in my opinion, is the right choice: A gradual
melting pot, which comes about organically and naturally.

This way does not ask anything of the state. The issues
with the state's initiating a melting pot policy are clear:
Who will decide what the preeminent cultural identity
should be? This is the question that caused many Middle
Eastern and North African Jews to feel discriminated
against, as their identity was ripped away by European
Jews who defined what the "right" culture was.

However, it is also wrong to encourage divisions within
the nation. Rather, one must let history do what it knows
best: With time, slowly, the nation itself will create a
new culture, which will include bits and pieces from the
different cultures that came together in Israel.

If a gradual and natural, organic evolution defines
"Israeli" culture, the result will be a blend of parts of
different subgroups' cultures. It might be a long process,
but it will ensure that historical evolution decides what
aspects of each culture survive, rather than a man with
limited intellect.

With time, a new culture will emerge: An authentic Israeli culture that is also a universal culture, incorporating aspects from all the different cultures of Israel's diverse population.

Tommy Lapid opposed the idea

At the beginning of this chapter, I showed that this new universal-nationalistic culture can already be seen in the music industry. It might be because music is one of the more organic expressions of cultural output and is less defined by intellectual choice.

Indeed, Riff Cohen, who is known worldwide, explained once that only in Israel can she create her special universal sound, since you can hear the different cultures mixing with and influencing each other.

When one hears Benayoun perform Tchaikovsky's Trio in A minor on an oud, it does not feel incongruent to hear a European song played with a Middle Eastern instrument—it feels Israeli.

Within this process is the realization of the words of God to Abraham: "I will make you into a great nation... And in you all the families of the earth will be blessed."

Only a nation that builds a particularistic identity ("a great nation") from universal sources ("all the families of the earth") can realize this goal.

Yet there are some who are against this development of a new national identity.

Tommy Lapid once said of Benayoun's music: "We didn't occupy [the Arab town of] Tulkarm; Tulkarm is occupying us." It is noteworthy that it was specifically Benayoun's music that bothered Lapid, and not purely Middle Eastern music. As long as Middle Eastern artists sang purely Middle Eastern music, he did not feel threatened. But once there was a mix of different cultural influences merged together to create a new music, and Middle Eastern influences became a defining part of Israeli culture, he could not accept this.

Multiculturalism did not bother him; the synthesis did.

Yet the nation is not controlled by the old elites trying to define what the right culture is, and it is specifically those artists who are able to merge different cultural influences who become successful in Israel.

About a year ago, Rotem Shefy and Liat Sebbag created a Middle Eastern cover to the song Karma Police, by Radiohead. What started as a musical experiment became an outstanding success, and in just a few weeks, the clip was viewed over 300,000 times on YouTube.

Everywhere one looks in Israel's music industry, one thing is clear: People are asking for a universal national identity.

This is the new Israeli identity.

The Sephardi Cultural Revival—A Critical Outlook

In recent years, we have witnessed a revival of Middle Eastern and Sephardi culture in Israel. In the early years of the Zionist Movement, Israel was faced with the critical question of how best to absorb immigrants from all over the world. As seen in the previous chapter, on the one hand, Ze'ev Jabotinsky wanted to adopt a liberal approach that would allow each demographic to maintain its special character.

David Ben-Gurion, on the other hand, sought to bring into being a new kind of Jew, by creating a new Israeli national identity to replace the various identities Jews brought with them from the Diaspora.

Since Mapai was the party in power when the state was established, government policy was aligned with Ben-Gurion's "melting pot" vision. Even those who supported the policy must have been aware of the side effects of this melting pot: Cultures that had evolved over thousands of years, whether in Arab or Western European countries, were destined to be eradicated.

Today, a strong national Israeli culture exists—with everyone speaking the same language, serving in the same army and fighting the same wars—and that common base already exists. So, it is not surprising that various movements have grown over the years seeking, each in its own way, to reconnect with the various cultural, family and community traditions of the Diaspora. Many of these movements have focused particularly on reviving Middle Eastern and North African cultures.

Many such formal action groups are missing the point of what is really behind the desire to restore Sephardi identity. The wider Sephardi community clearly wishes to combat the suppression of its culture in the melting pot, and to achieve new recognition of the value of Sephardi ethnic identity. But those who raise this flag do not represent the will of the Sephardi mass public. In my humble opinion, this gap is due to the fact that the models of philosophical thought upon which these movements are based bear no relation to the real desires of the majority of the Sephardi community.

Is the Sephardi cultural revival a postmodern movement?

Most of the new organizations advocating for Sephardi cultural revival base themselves on the foundations of postmodernism.

The postmodernists ask specific questions in the field of philosophy; they move away from questions of content, such as "What is true?" "What is false?" and "What are the correct and incorrect ways to behave?" Instead, they ask: "Who decides?" "Who rules?" and "What is the purpose of this controlling power?" These questions lead to deconstruction and an attempt to break up the established framework.

The postmodern approach was already applied historically to the Middle Eastern conflict, when Palestinian—

American literary theorist Edward Said, observing the Western hold over Middle Eastern Arabs and ascribing it to self-serving reasons, claimed that the West oppressed the Arab population. From his standpoint: "Were it not for the wicked imperialists, racists and Zionists, the Arab world could return to its former greatness." Said's theory is the platform for the post-Zionist movements that flourished on a similar foundation, such as the movement led in the academic world by Ilan Pappé.

Many of the existing movements promoting Sephardi interests model themselves on the teachings of Said, claiming that here, too, that one group is controlled by another—as the Zionist Ashkenazi elite exerts a hegemonic influence over the deprived Sephardi minority. In her book *Towards Multicultural Thinking*, Ella Shohat asserts that "recognition of the exploitation of the Sephardic community and impoverishment of their culture justifies an indictment against Zionism and Israel." The post-colonial attitude that Shohat nurtured, based on the views of Said, was adopted by the intellectual leaders of the new Sephardi revival organizations, including Yehouda Shenhav, Yossi Yonah and others.

Such an approach can have only one outcome: Opposition to the controlling group in order to restore power to the deprived. This gave birth to a situation in which the pro-Sephardi movements can be viewed as both anti-Zionist and anti-Ashkenazi. Accordingly, Arie Kizel of the University of Haifa, concluded one of his articles with the following statement: "The new pro-Sephardic debate is subversive, destructive and working against the national interest, which it sees primarily as a colonialist-Orientalist-ethnic-Ashkenazi project."

It is little wonder that Yossi Yonah of the Democratic Sephardi Coalition, now a Zionist Union MK, spoke out in opposition to the term Zionism: "I admit that I do not identify with that word, 'Zionism.' It does not express who I am," he said in a Haaretz interview.

The most difficult problem presented by these movements, alongside the moral or factual questions, is that they do not really represent Israel's Sephardi community, the overwhelming majority of which is comprised of nationalists and Zionists. When Yonah states that he was once a Zionist, it is because he probably grew up in a Zionist home—like most members of the Sephardi community. Sephardim are proud of their children's military service, love the State of Israel and feel Zionist in every way. From an electoral point of view, they tend to vote Center-Right, and not the far-Left that these new organizations represent.

There is a real movement for people to reconnect with the Jewish traditions of North Africa and the Middle East—a movement characterized by the revival of the study of traditional religious melodies (*piyutim*), the opening of Middle Eastern style entertainment venues and, in the religious world, the study of the North African sages' teachings. Thus, a situation has arisen in which a movement exists, but its purported delegates do not actually represent its constituents at all.

The Sephardi cultural revival as a conservative movement

I believe there is a more suitable framework for the Sephardi movement that would be more representative of the aspirations of the Sephardi population. It is the opposite of the postmodernist movement—and it is the political conservatism movement.

The basic principles of conservatism assert that one man alone, however wise, cannot create structures that will be more effective than those already established. Therefore, conservatives oppose the dismantling of the social bodies and structures that postmodernists seek to destroy and prefer to maintain their loyalty to existing traditions.

Conservatives will try to make improvements and institute change, but always within the established framework.

It is not always easy to understand the logic behind our social institutions; just as often, we find it hard to fathom the nature of our existing customs. This reflects a limitation in our thinking rather than evidence that such institutions and customs are incorrect. Tradition, the accumulated wisdom of the ages, is better than the wisdom of any one person.

Conservatives respect existing institutions and find value in the different frameworks within which we live: the family, the community and the nation. Similarly, the Sephardi people revere these institutions—in contrast to the postmodernists, who seek to destroy them. So, a conservative is loyal to his nation, as is the nationalist Sephardi Jew, who respects both his Israeli national identity and the Zionist movement.

Conservatives oppose the dismantling of existing frameworks. In the words of Edmund Burke, the father of the conservative movement, "It is with infinite caution that any man ought to venture upon pulling down an edifice."

Conservatives tend to shy away from drastic change and to prefer continuity; in the same way, the traditional Sephardi culture is reluctant to destroy the mainstays of its belief system and prefers continuity.

Such an affirmative approach to religion is also more likely to find a natural home among conservative intellectuals than among the postmodernists. Burke claims that "religion is the basis of civil society, and the source of all good and of all comfort."

Conservatives respect all identities and view them as important; an outlook that is well-attuned to Sephardi yearnings to reconnect with their roots through the ancestral traditions in which they were raised.

The movements to preserve Sephardi culture by a conservative approach could create a new cultural model that is more relevant than the postmodernist Sephardi movement: The focus would no longer be on hatred of Ashkenazim, but rather on love of the unique traditions of Sephardi Jewry. Resistance to oppression of the Sephardi traditions would remain but it would no longer issue from opposition to Zionism, rather from their love of those traditions—which also includes a love of Israel and the quest for a return of the exiled to Zion.

Such a description is more authentic than the postmodern description of Sephardi culture, as it represents the underlying feelings of many Sephardi people who wish to reconnect with the ways of their fathers.

It would be an excellent thing if the Sephardi movements begin to base their activities on the love of tradition, the Land of Israel and the State of Israel, instead of on a hatred of the "Ashkenazi brand of Zionism."

CONCLUSION

The chapters in this book, based on articles written in various publications over the past few years, span a number of topics.

From foreign to domestic policy, some more theoretical while others much more practical, they all have a common foundation: a conservative outlook on Israel's policies.

President Ronald Reagan famously described conservative philosophy, and right-wing politics as a whole, as a "three-legged stool". In that analogy, the three legs of the conservative stool were the following: social conservatism, fiscal conservatism and strong national defense.

Social conservatism is first and foremost recognition that age-old values are in fact valuable, and that we should not quickly reject them based on a theoretical postmodernist deconstruction. The values and institutions that make up society are important and their disintegration could cause the disintegration of our society as a whole.

Fiscal conservatism stems from a belief in freedom and the free market, and the belief that government intervention in business is usually a bad thing. Therefore, a fiscal conservative looks to lower taxes, remove regulations and puts trust in the individual rather than in the state.

On foreign affairs, conservatives believe in a strong national defense as a way to ensure the continued security of one's people. This realist philosophy opposes opposes utopic visions of sacrificing security for an intangible promise of peace. Peace will come when our enemies know they cannot defeat us.

While writing the articles that make up this book, I asked myself repeatedly if Israel even had such a conservative movement. Does Israel even have a right wing?

On the one hand, Israel does have social conservatives, and foreign affairs hawks. It even has some (although too few) fiscal conservatives.

However, almost no one in Israel embraces this three-legged stool as a coherent message.

This book is an attempt to translate the three-legged stool analogy into a language relevant to Israel. By basing myself on the Israeli national anthem, I suggest Israel's conservative movement should base itself on these three legs:

A Free: A love of freedom, the free market and democracy, that promotes fiscal conservative values.

Nation: A belief in national pride and identity, a rejection of post-modernist tendencies to deconstruct such identities, and a belief in the age-old values of that nation. This promotes social conservative values in a way attuned to Israeli society.

In Our Land: Not only a love of the land of Israel but also a hawkish view of foreign policy that rejects territorial concessions based on the false promise of utopic peace with our neighbors, and prefers relying on a powerful military in order to ensure peace and quiet. This promotes a conservative view of foreign policy.

A love of freedom, a belief in national pride and identity and a hawkish view of foreign policy opposed to utopic visions of international relations—this is Israel's three-legged stool.

Israel is a young country that has accomplished incredible things in less than 70 years. As I hope I showed in this book, if Israel sticks to these important values, it will only keep growing and reaching even greater heights.

"Dan Illouz is a brilliant and honest commentator"
Ambassador Daniel Gal

"Dan is a man of values and a Zionist committed to the Jewish and democratic values that lie at the foundation of the State of Israel."
MK Naftali Bennet, Minister of Education

Cover Design: 'Bein-Hashurot', SHEKEL graphic studio
Pictures: Shutterstock and Freepik